FIFTH EDITION

SECRETS

· · · · · · · · · ·

of

· · · · · · · · · ·

GREAT ESTATE PLANNING

BRENDA GEIGER, J.D.

WORD ASSOCIATION PUBLISHERS
www.wordassociation.com
1.800.827.7903

GEIGER LAW OFFICE, P.C.
1917 Palomar Oaks Way, Suite 160
Carlsbad, CA 92008

(760) 448-2220
www.geigerlawoffice.com

Copyright © 2024, 2022, 2018, 2016, 2014 by Brenda Geiger.

FIFTH EDITION

Published 2024

Printed in the United States of America.

ISBN: 978-1-63385-516-8 [paperback]
ISBN: 978-1-63385-517-5 [hardback]

Designed and published by

Word Association Publishers
205 Fifth Avenue
Tarentum, Pennsylvania 15084

www.wordassociation.com
1.800.827.7903

Disclaimer

This book is not intended to be legal advice. The information contained within this book is for educational purposes only. Before making any legal decisions, you should first consult a qualified attorney.

Contents

1. What is Estate Planning? 1

2. What is a Probate? 3

3. The Estate Planning Process.. 7

4. What is the Difference between a Will and a Trust? 11

5. How to Fund Your Revocable Trust 15

6. Estate & Gift Taxes... 21

7. Marital Planning in the Joint Trust: Balancing Income
   Tax, Transfer Tax, and Asset Protection Concerns 25

8. Creditor Protection for Your Child's Inheritance............... 41

9. Nominating a Guardian for a Minor Child....................... 47

10. Protecting Your Retirement Accounts for Your Children
    with a Retirement Protector Trust™.................................. 55

11. Why LLCs Make for Great Asset Protection
    for Your Rental Real Estate 63

12. Protecting Part of Your Net Worth with a Domestic
    Asset Protection Trust 69

13. Planning for the Long Term Care of an Elderly Parent...... 79

14. What is Trust Administration and What Does a
    Successor Trustee Do? 85

15. Advanced Estate Planning Strategies 91

16. The Top 25 Estate Planning Mistakes People
    Make and How to Avoid Them... 105

17. What to Do Next? 129

18. About the Author 131

one

What is Estate Planning?

Estate planning is about deciding in advance who will be in control of your health care decisions and your assets in the event of your incapacity or death. For example, if you are incapacitated, you will need someone that can make financial and medical decisions for you. Unless you want to have the courts interfere, this is accomplished by having a successor Trustee set up through a revocable trust, a designated Power of Attorney agent for other financial related situations and a Health Care Directive agent. It's also recommended to have a backup Trustee and agents after your first choices.

Revocable trusts serve many purposes. If you are incapacitated, they allow a successor Trustee you have pre-selected to step into your shoes and conduct trust business almost exclusively without a hitch. Some things they might do while you are incapacitated are pay your bills and take care of you and your children financially. At death, your successor Trustee performs what we call Trust Administration. This is, in basic terms, the process of paying all of your debts and creditors and then distributing the remaining assets to your beneficiaries in the manner you have prescribed. For more details on Trust Administration, see chapter 14 on "What is *if you are incapacitated, you will need someone that can make financial and medical decisions for you*

Trust Administration and What Does a Successor Trustee Do?"

The Power of Attorney agent, listed in your Durable Power of Attorney document, handles tax, financial and legal matters that fall outside the realm of your trust. Depending upon how the Power of Attorney is drafted, a Power of Attorney agent might hold the power to file your tax returns, execute a Disclaimer on your behalf, access your retirement accounts, file legal actions on your behalf, or even manage your digital assets. Most Power of Attorney documents are drafted to take effect upon declaration of your incapacity by a doctor, but some are drafted to take effect immediately after being signed. The latter is more common when a life-threatening illness presents itself or we have an elderly person who needs assistance immediately.

The Advance Health Care Directive (as we call it in California) allows us to pick who will make medical decisions for us if we are unable to do so for ourselves, choose end-of-life decisions and opt-in to being an organ donor. This too can be made to be effective immediately so that family members do not have to wait for an incapacity declaration to help make decisions for a loved one.

two

What Is a Probate?

In a nutshell, probate is the process of gathering up all of a deceased person's property and recording all of their debts and creditors with the court. After an Order by the Court is made as to the payment of all debts and creditors, the remainder of the decedent's property is then ordered to be distributed to either the decedent's beneficiaries in his or her will or to his or her "heirs at law" under the California Probate statute (if no will exists).

If probate is necessary, there will need to be someone in charge as Executor. If the deceased had a will, that will is filed with a Petition at the Probate Court and the will names an Executor. But if the decedent had no will, then a family member usually petitions the court to be appointed as the "Executor" or "Administrator" of the estate. Most of the time, if there are no objections by other family members, the court will appoint the petitioner as Executor.

The process of probate in California typically lasts 16-24 months depending on the County where you are filing in and the current case load of the court. All probate filings are also open to public inspection, and it can be expensive. For example, the statutory fees to the Executor and attorney on a $1,000,000 estate are $46,000 plus filing and other court related fees.

The first step in a probate is for the Executor to file the will and a "Petition for Probate" with the probate court in the county where the deceased person lived or died as well as pay a filing fee. Notice to heirs of the decedent and beneficiaries under the will are also part of the process. The will must also be proved up (shown to be valid). When the initial requirements have been met, then the court issues what are called "Letters Testamentary" or "Letters of Administration." The Letters officially appoint the Executor and give that person authority to act with regard to the estate assets. Legal notice to all known creditors and a publication of the probate in a local newspaper must also be given.

The Executor will need to marshal all of the decedent's assets, track down their outstanding bills and creditors and report this information to the Court. A Probate Referee is assigned to the case and he or she must value all of the deceased person's property and that information gets filed with the Court. The probate referee must also be paid for their services. A tax identification number (EIN) also needs to be obtained for the probate estate for income tax filing purposes and a bank account in the name of the probate estate needs to be opened. Good record keeping by the Executor is a must.

The Executor should consider hiring an experienced estate attorney who understands the process and can represent them in Court. Most probates in California are handled under the state's Independent Administration of Estates Act. This lets the Executor handle most estate matters without having to get prior permission from the probate court. Some of the things an Executor might do are sell property, pay taxes, and approve or reject claims from creditors without court supervision.

The Executor also has a duty to keep all of the decedent's property safe. This might mean securing a home and maintaining homeowner's insurance or moving valuables to a safety deposit box or secure storage unit so they are not stolen.

The Executor also has a duty to keep all of the decedent's property safe.

When all bills, creditors and taxes have been paid from the probate estate and an accounting has been filed, the executor petitions the court to close the estate and relieve them of their legal duty by discharging them. Then, the executor can distribute all the estate assets to the people who are to inherit them (either the beneficiaries listed in the decedent's will or to the decedent's heirs at law under the state statute).

Lastly, the Executor and attorney who filed the probate are each entitled to a statutory fee as laid out in the California Probate code (and in some instances for extra fees called

"Extraordinary" fees if additional legal services were necessary in the probate). The statutory fees are 4% on the first $100,000 of FMV to the Executor and the attorney; 3% each to the attorney and Executor on the next $100,000; and 2% each on the next value between $200,000 and $1,000,000. The percentage scales down on amounts over $1,000,000. It is important to note that the statutory fees are based on the *fair market value* of the assets in probate, not the equity in the assets. This is why it is typically far less expensive to administer a trust privately as compared to probating an estate via a will or through an intestate probate if no will exists. And it is usually a lot less stressful for the tustee to administer a trust than an executor to administer a probate action.

three

The Estate Planning Process

Now that you know what each of the major estate planning documents are and what they do, as well as the fact that trusts can help you avoid Probate, let's look at what the process of estate planning is. Generally, estate planning in our office happens in a three-step process. The first step is called the design meeting. The design meeting is conducted after we've received and reviewed your estate plan fact finder and existing trust (if you have one). We usually require this at least one week prior to our first meeting so that our attorneys can maximize their time with you and you get the most benefit out of the meeting. We use the information from your fact finder and your existing trust to tailor the design meeting for you. If you have a current trust, we will also be discussing our legal opinions and recommendations with you regarding your existing trust and any other estate planning documents you have provided us with.

At your design meeting, your attorney will examine what your goals are and what your hopes are for your family in the future. We'll also be discussing things like who your Trustee should be, who your power of attorney and health *we examine what your goals are and what your hopes are for your family in the future*

care agents should be, and who to name as permanent and temporary Guardian for your children (if you have minors) if something should happen to you. We'll also be talking about how your assets should pass to your spouse, children and/or other beneficiaries. Other beneficiaries could be other family members, friends or charities. Another part of the design process is to look at what happens when one spouse passes away and how the assets can be passed to your spouse. (See Chapter 7 for more details).

In the chapters that follow, we will be discussing not only how property can be left to a spouse but how you can leave assets to your children or other beneficiaries in a way that protects them from creditors, predators and divorcing spouses. In your design meeting, we also discuss your health care directive options and the purpose of having a HIPAA Authorization for Release of Medical Information. These documents are critical in an estate plan so that if you're ever injured or ill and cannot make medical decisions for yourself, your family or other designated people can step in and make medical decisions for you.

The second step in our estate planning process is your signing meeting. This usually occurs about 3-4 weeks after your initial design meeting with your attorney. Before you come in for your trust signing meeting, we will send you your trust summary, Advance Health Care Directive, your names and fiduciaries list (to ensure we have all names properly spelled and in the right order) and your Guardianship Nomination (if you have minor children). At the signing meeting, you will be signing your trust (or trust restatement) and your other estate planning documents. You will need to bring your passport, driver's license or other legal identification for the notary. The signing meeting usually takes between 45 minutes to an hour. At the end of the signing meeting, we will schedule a third meeting with you called your funding meeting. At the funding meeting (which is usually about 3-4 weeks later) your designated legal assistant reviews the process of funding your trust with you and provides you with your funding tool kit so that you can coordinate with banks and other financial institutions regarding your assets.

Our team makes the process with us easy and simple and all with a kind smile and professionalism.

four

What is the Difference between a Will and a Trust?

Wills and Trusts are similar in that both are legal vehicles for passing assets at death and can each be amended throughout the will or trust maker's lifetime. However, the differences are far greater. Wills must be submitted to the probate court and proved up (proven to be valid), and therefore require court supervision in order to pass the decedent's assets to their beneficiaries. Further, a will is a death-time document and has no legal effect during the will maker's incapacity.

Revocable trusts, on the other hand, are living documents that can be designed to protect the trust Grantor while they are incapacitated from a conservatorship. A conservatorship is a court process where a person is placed by the court to manage your finances and/or your healthcare. Trusts also do not go through the probate process, they preserve privacy upon administration, and are typically far less costly in terms of trust administration costs as compared to typical probate fees in California.

The avoidance of a conservatorship over the estate of an incapacitated person is preferred. A properly drafted revocable trust can help the trust maker avoid a later conservatorship by assigning a Trustee to make financial decisions about the trust assets and to pay the trust maker's bills and medical expenses if they are unable to personally. Conservatorships are also expensive and require court supervision and accounting. The court may also place someone you never envisioned being in charge of your financial or medical affairs. So, it is best to designate a successor Trustee through a revocable trust and have a power of attorney agent (which is often the same person as the successor Trustee).

Wills are also subject to public inspection. This is not advantageous because of the lack of privacy. The whole world will be put on notice as to what assets you owned at death, who your creditors were and to whom you left your assets. Another danger attendant of the will becoming public knowledge is that the Executor could be approached by unscrupulous investment firms and taken advantage of. Trusts are private documents and afford the Grantor a shield from the outside world's prying eyes.

In California, a typical will probate can take from 16-24 months on average. This is because the court systems are overcrowded due to budget cuts. For example, in September of 2012, the North County San Diego Probate Court was closed, and all probate matters were moved to the San Diego Central Probate Court in downtown San Diego. On the other hand, a simple trust administration can take far less time but for larger estates that are complex (i.e., estates subject to estate tax or contain unusual assets), it could take longer but still usually less time than a probate.

Wills are also subject to public inspection.

Will probates also cost far more than the cost involved with a trust administration. For example, a probate on a $1,000,000 estate would be over $46,000 for the probate statutory and filing fees to the executor and the attorney. The fees on a probate case are calculated on the gross value of the estate, not taking into account the debt against any of the property. Therefore, you could have a house that is worth $1,000,000 that has a loan against it for $800,000, yet the statutory fees are calculated on $1,000,000, not the $200,000 of equity. Trust administration fees on the other hand are typically far less. They vary based on the complexity and size of the estate, but they are almost always substantially less than the fees for probate.

five

How to Fund Your Revocable Trust

First of all, let's explain what it means to "fund" your revocable trust since this terminology tends to confuse a lot of people. Funding your trust simply means putting assets into the name of your trust and coordinating the beneficiary forms on your life insurance and retirement accounts to match your estate planning intent.

To give you a concrete example, let's say that you have a house, a checking account, a savings account, a non-retirement brokerage account, a 401K, an IRA, and two life insurance policies. The house, checking account, savings account, and brokerage account would all need to be re-titled to be owned by your trust. Typically, in a revocable trust, the person or persons who set up the trust (the Grantors) are also the Trustees (the ones who control the assets of the trust). The house gets transferred to the trust through a deed that gets recorded with the county recorder's office. The bank accounts require you to go to the bank and request that the accounts are titled in your name as Trustee of your revocable trust. This is fairly simple and if you are working with us, we will give you a nice funding letter and copy of your certification of trust to help you in the process.

The brokerage account gets re-titled in the name of your trust either by your financial advisor or by contacting the custodian of your brokerage account directly and requesting the transfer. Or they may send you the form they need you to fill out, sign and return to make sure the account gets transferred to your trust.

For retirement accounts, you should never transfer ownership to your revocable trust. These types of assets must be owned by an individual per IRS rules. However, you can update your beneficiary form to coordinate with the intent of your trust. This is where legal advice becomes really important. There are a few mistakes we have seen people make and there are decisions you will need to make as to where your retirement accounts go should you pass away. In most cases, leaving a qualified retirement account to a spouse makes the most sense for what is trying to be accomplished and for tax planning purposes. There are things a spouse can do with the retirement account that other beneficiaries simply cannot do as well. But you should always list a contingent beneficiary of your retirement plans. The options here might be to list children, charity, other family members, your revocable trust (provided you have the right provisions in your trust), or to a Retirement Protector Trust™ for creditor protection.

Note that because making the proper beneficiary designation is so important for retirement accounts and may involve many complex tax and individual family issues, consultation with an attorney skilled in this area of the law is highly recommended. Once you have executed a new beneficiary designation form for each of your retirement accounts and you have returned them to your plan custodians, *For retirement accounts, you should never transfer ownership to your revocable trust.* they should return to you a letter confirming the change of beneficiaries. You should place a copy of the confirmation letters under your TRUST ASSETS tab in your estate plan portfolio (trust plan binder). Important note: you should never list a minor child as the primary or contingent beneficiary of your retirement account. If you do, the court will need to appoint a guardian at litem to take custody of the account until the minor reaches the age of 18. The revocable trust (if properly drafted with "conduit" provisions for retirement accounts) is the better option when minors are involved as primary or contingent beneficiaries. The Trustee can take over management of the retirement account and stretch out the account for maximum deferral benefits for the minor beneficiary. For more information on asset protection for retirement accounts, see Chapter 10 on "Stretching Out and Protecting Your Retirement Account for Your Children with a Retirement Protector Trust™".

If you do not have an estate that is subject to the estate tax (remember to include life insurance policies in your name as part of your gross estate for estate tax calculation purposes), it is perfectly fine to list your revocable trust as the beneficiary of your life insurance. However, careful crafting of your trust is part of this process. I will give you an example to highlight this. Let's say clients Jane and John come to my office and tell me that they are married but that this is a second marriage for each of them. Further, they tell me that Jane has a 9-year-old child from a prior marriage and that her ex-husband has a traumatic brain injury (TBI) and would not be capable of supporting his daughter if Jane died. Jane and John also just had a baby together. Jane is worried that her daughter from her prior marriage might not be cared for in the way she wishes if she died. In this particular situation, a separate trust that has a life insurance policy listing the separate trust as the beneficiary, and that is owned by Jane, is a good solution to meet her objectives. Jane's other life insurance policy lists her joint revocable trust with John as the primary beneficiary so that John will have immediate access to the money through their joint trust if something happened to Jane. John also listed the joint trust as the beneficiary of his life insurance policy. Both Jane's daughter from a prior marriage and their new baby together are the beneficiaries of their joint trust in the event both Jane and John die together.

The reason I pointed out this more complex set of circumstances is to highlight that it is not always a clear-cut decision. In general, however, if we have a first-time married couple with minor children, it may be best to list the revocable trust as the beneficiary of the life insurance policy, not the spouse (depending on the marital tax provisions set up in the trust). If you do so, your revocable trust terms will govern what happens to the policy proceeds if you die. It is advisable for you to contact the insurance agent or company that sold you the policy to ensure that the proper paperwork is filled out and signed to change the beneficiary or add your trust as a contingent beneficiary after your spouse. If you have children, this is particularly important. We have often seen parents of minor children list their spouse as primary and their minor children as the contingent beneficiaries. The problem with this is that it will force court intervention. No insurance company will willingly write a large check to a person under the age of 18. This means a guardianship needs to be created and the guardian approved by the court must make annual accountings to the court regarding the insurance proceeds, in most cases. Guardianships are long, expensive and they lack private control. Even worse, the money is not even protected once the child reaches 18 from their immature decisions or from their creditors. He or she could take the money, go on a shopping spree or just fritter it away and skip college. These are all bad things that with simple estate planning can be avoided.

six

Estate & Gift Taxes

Effective as of January 1, 2018, the Tax Cuts and Jobs Act of 2017 changed the Federal Estate Tax exemption rate. In 2024, that exemption has now risen to $13,610,000 per person (indexed for inflation). This number represents the unified credit amount that each U.S. Citizen can gift during their lifetime, transfer at death or apply to generation-skipping transfers. It's all under one unified credit. For example, if Tom gave his child $2MM during his lifetime, his credit would be reduced to $11,610,000 if he died in 2024 for death time and/or generation-skipping transfers.

Estate, Gift and Generation-Skipping Transfer Taxes

Under the current law, the estate tax and gift tax rates are unified (made the same). This means that the estate and gift taxes create a single graduated exemption rate schedule for both estate and gift taxes. The single lifetime exemption can be used for lifetime gifts, death time bequests and generation-skipping transfers. The top estate and gift tax rate is 40%. The Federal exemption for estate and gift transfers is $13,610,000 per person for 2024 and is indexed annually for inflation. What this means is that in 2024, each U.S. citizen may transfer up to $13,610,000 throughout his or her lifetime or at death (or some combination thereof) and not be subject to estate or gift taxes. The exemption that applies to a decedent is the exemption that is in effect in the year he or she dies.

A married couple with community property assets may transfer up to $27,220,000 as of 2024 since each spouse has their own exemption. Special rules apply for estates involving non-US citizen spouses, so consultation with an experienced estate planning attorney is strongly recommended.

The annual gift tax exclusion amount for 2024 is $18,000 per recipient. A married couple may gift split $36,000 per recipient from their community property. Gifts beyond the $36,000 married, or $18,000 single exclusion amounts in 2024 require the filing of a 709-gift tax return to record the gift with the IRS.

If the person making the 709 gift has not used up his or her entire $13,610,000 unified credit (2024), no gift tax will be due. The IRS just requires you to record the gift through the filing of a 709-gift tax return. If, however, you have used up your unified credit on prior gifts, you will need to pay gift taxes on the gift that is made if it is over the $18,000 (single) or $36,000 (married gift split) annual gift tax exclusion amount. For more information on gifting and gifting trusts, see Chapter 15 "Advanced Estate Planning Strategies" in this book, or my book "Estate Planning Secrets of the Affluent

Third Edition" (Word Association Press) available through our office, Amazon and Barnes and Noble.

Also, as of this writing, the current estate and gift tax exemption will sunset on December 31, 2025. On January 1, 2026, if no legislation has passed modifying the exemption, it will fall back to $5,000,000 per person with an index for inflation. Many tax experts estimate that the indexed exemption in 2026 will be around $7,000,000 per person.

seven

Marital Planning in the Joint Trust: Balancing Income Tax, Transfer Tax, and Asset Protection Concerns

Marital planning in the joint trust context can be complex. This chapter examines the tax and non-tax implications of five main marital options upon the death of the first spouse. The options we will explore are: (1) leaving all property to a spouse in a survivor's trust; (2) dividing the property into an A trust and B trust after the death of the first spouse; (3) leaving all of the deceased spouse's property to the surviving spouse and including provisions for the surviving spouse to disclaim to a Bypass trust; (4) leaving the surviving spouse's interest in the trust in a survivor's trust at the death of the first spouse and the decedent's interest in a QTIP marital trust for the benefit of the surviving spouse; and (5) using a Clayton election after the death of the first spouse to plan for the possibility of estate taxes and to protect the surviving spouse and eventual heirs of the decedent.

The five approaches outlined above are the most common forms of marital planning in the joint trust, but they often apply to separate trusts in separate property states for married couples as well.

All to the Surviving Spouse:

The first option is the simplest. If husband and wife so desire, they can leave everything to the surviving spouse either outright or in further trust in a survivor's trust. Directing property to a Survivor's trust would allow the trust to continue without requiring the surviving spouse to later create a new individual trust after the death of the first spouse. With this option, the surviving spouse has full control over the trust property left to them by the deceased spouse. The surviving spouse may change the plan later by revoking or amending the trust.

For federal estate tax purposes, the entire trust estate is includible in the surviving spouse's estate. If only one spouse's estate tax exclusion is needed to shelter the entire estate, this may be a viable option for the couple. But other non-tax issues must be assessed as discussed below. The property owned in the survivor's trust at the death of the surviving spouse also receives a basis adjustment when the remainder beneficiaries later inherit.

This type of plan is simple and effective, but it does have drawbacks. If the surviving spouse later remarries, nothing prevents them from changing the beneficiaries of the trust to the new spouse or the new spouse's children, or from terminating the trust and moving the assets to a joint trust with the new spouse. Those assets could be later taken in a divorce with the new spouse.

There is also no asset protection for the surviving spouse over the deceased spouse's share, the assets may be used to satisfy judgments in lawsuits, are accessible to creditors, and may be included in a bankruptcy. But where husband and wife have a long, stable, single marriage, a smaller estate, and are not concerned with asset protection or remarriage issues, this may be a viable option. (One postmortem strategy may include porting the deceased spouse's unused exemption amount through a portability election on a 706 Federal Estate Tax return, even when the estate is nontaxable in case the estate tax exemption goes down later.)

A/B Trusts:

The second option is to divide the trust estate into an A and a B trust through various marital deduction funding formulas. These formulas include the pecuniary marital formula, fractional marital formula, and the pecuniary credit shelter formula. Each approach divides the decedent's estate into shares at his or her death, often creating a share covered by all or part of the decedent's available Estate tax Exemption amount, and another share covered by the unlimited marital deduction. Because these are mandatory funding formulas, the surviving spouse _must_ divide the trust according to the formula at the death of the first spouse, creating two trusts.

Years ago, this form of marital planning was quite common because the estate tax exemption was so low. The main driver for this type of plan was the desire to use each spouse's federal estate tax exemption (and often, where applicable, a state estate tax exemption). The surviving spouse's half would be applied to the Survivor's trust and the deceased spouse's half up to the exemption amount would fund to a Bypass trust.

When the federal estate tax exemption was fairly low, many families in America were motivated to establish mandatory marital deduction formula-based estate plans such as this. For example, in 2001, the federal estate tax exemption was $675,000 with a top tax rate of 55%. With life insurance owned in the name of the decedent included in this exemption calculation, many couples were almost forced into A/B trust planning to plan for estate taxes.

Today, with the option for a portability election on the 706-estate tax return at the death of the first spouse, the exemption can be used by a surviving spouse after the first spouse dies. But there are some drawbacks and limitations to relying on portability alone such as loss of the ported exemption if the surviving spouse later remarries.

Also from an income tax perspective, creation of a Bypass trust at the death of the first spouse has some drawbacks. Assets funded into the Bypass trust receive a capital gains tax basis measured at the date of death of the first spouse to die, and do not later receive another basis adjustment when the survivor dies. For example, if a piece of real estate valued at $2MM at the death of the first spouse is funded into the Bypass trust and remains there until the survivor later dies, any increase in value from the first spouse's death until the date of death of the surviving spouse would be subject to capital gains tax liability upon sale, by the remainder trust beneficiaries.

This result can be avoided with creative planning, but the client must be advised of the income tax implications. For instance, if the surviving spouse sells the property from the Bypass trust in exchange for a note, or if the survivor replaced it with other assets not subject to gain, the income tax problem can be mitigated.

Today, much of the planning around mandatory A/B marital trusts involves larger estates. It may also enter the planning conversation where a spouse wants to ensure the eventual remainder beneficiaries originally chosen by the couple are not later disinherited by the surviving spouse. And often spouses seek asset protection for the surviving spouse from creditors, predators, and future divorcing spouses.

The Marital Disclaimer Approach:

A third option is to design the trust to pass all of the trust assets to the surviving spouse or in a survivor's trust and reserve the option for the surviving spouse to disclaim all or a portion of the decedent's share to a B (Bypass trust). A disclaimer is a refusal by someone to accept property that they are otherwise due to receive. The person signing the disclaimer (the "disclaimant") makes an irrevocable and unqualified decision to refuse any interest in the disclaimed property. The disclaimer must comply with federal and state law. This type of planning is often referred to as "disclaimer trust" planning.

The disclaimer trust is a common form of "wait and see" tax planning for married couples. They may want to defer the decision to use a Bypass trust for estate tax purposes or for asset protection for the surviving spouse. In a disclaimer trust plan, the surviving spouse *may* decide to disclaim property left to them by their spouse in trust, but they are not *required* to do so. If the surviving spouse disclaims property received from the deceased spouse, the disclaimed property is transferred to the Bypass trust. A valid disclaimer must be executed within nine (9) months of the date of death of the first spouse.

The Bypass trust is typically drafted so that the surviving spouse manages it as Trustee and has access to income (and often principal, limited to the ascertainable standard of health, education, maintenance, and support, or "HEMS"). As an exception under IRC §2518(b)(4)(A), the surviving spouse may benefit from the disclaimed assets in the Bypass trust, but the assets are not included in the survivor's gross estate when they die. If it were not for this, and possible asset protection of the disclaimed assets (depending on state law and the timing of the disclaimer), there would be little reason for a surviving spouse to disclaim. At the death of the first spouse, if the survivor desires asset protection for the assets disclaimed, creation of the Bypass trust may make sense if the assets being disclaimed are not likely to trigger a later taxable gain, and even if the deceased's spouse's unified credit is not needed to mitigate estate tax.

The key advantage to this type of plan is the ability to later assess the estate at the death of the first to die. The decision can be made then to create a Bypass trust if the estate has grown significantly, if the estate tax exemption has decreased, or where asset protection is desired for the deceased spouse's share of the assets. The spouse may also decide to file a 706 and claim portability for some or all of the deceased spouse's Unused Exclusion Amount (DSUEA).

If the surviving spouse appoints a third-party independent trustee over the Bypass trust, the trust may contain a broader, non-ascertainable distribution standard, further increasing the asset protection for the Bypass trust assets for the spouse and remainder beneficiaries.

The key advantage to this type of plan is the ability to assess the estate at the death of the first to die.

The obvious problem with a disclaimer trust plan is that the surviving spouse may fail to disclaim when it makes the most sense. They may also fail to disclaim because they do not obtain sound legal advice. This point becomes even more poignant when there is a blended family. The surviving spouse may later change his or her mind and decide not to disclaim the decedent's assets to a Bypass trust. Those assets may then be given to other beneficiaries that were never intended when the couple first established their plan, such as to a new spouse.

The surviving spouse may also accidentally void the opportunity to disclaim. There are specific state and federal requirements that must be followed in order to make an effective disclaimer. For example, a disclaimer can fail if the surviving spouse manipulates the decedent's assets in any way that constitutes acceptance of the property before the disclaimer is made. This could happen if the surviving spouse moved the property from one account to another or sold the property and replaced it with another asset, for example. It could also happen if the surviving spouse fails to execute the disclaimer within the nine (9) month window.

Survivor's Trust/QTIP Trust Plan:

The fourth type of marital formula for a joint trust is the Survivor's Trust/QTIP Trust Plan. This formula uses a forced Survivor's Trust and QTIP Marital Trust split at the death of the first spouse. The separate property of the surviving spouse (if any) and half of the community property in the trust are to be funded to a Survivor's Trust at the death of the first spouse and the deceased spouse's separate property (if any) and half of the community property are funded to a QTIP Marital Trust for the benefit of the surviving spouse during their lifetime. After the death of the surviving spouse, the assets that remain in the QTIP Trust are distributed to the beneficiaries the couple chose together. If the surviving spouse doesn't amend the Survivor's Trust, the assets of that trust will also be distributed to the beneficiaries that the couple selected together and named in the trust.

There are several advantages to this type of trust plan. First, all of the property in both trusts receive a step-up in cost basis at the death of the surviving spouse and therefore avoid capital gains tax for your children or other beneficiaries. What this means is that any assets that are subject to capital gains (for example, real estate, stock accounts, business interests, etc.) would have a new cost basis as of the date of death of the surviving spouse for the assets in not only the Survivor's Trust but in the QTIP Trust as well. Additionally, the QTIP Marital Trust can add a measure of asset protection for the surviving spouse over the QTIP assets in the event of a lawsuit or bankruptcy where an independent Trustee is serving and protect the assets from a new spouse. The QTIP Marital Trust is also ideal for those who wish to maintain certainty that their children or other beneficiaries will eventually inherit their portion of the estate after the death of the surviving spouse.

The one potential disadvantage in general is that there would be two sub-trusts instead of one at the death of the first spouse and the requirement to file a 706-death tax return to elect QTIP treatment over the assets being funded to the QTIP Marital Trust. The QTIP election must be made by an independent executor at the death of the first spouse within 9 months of date of death, but this period is extendible by 6 months. The surviving spouse can appoint their attorney or CPA to make the election through the decedent's Will.

To illustrate how this type of plan works practically, imagine Bob and Jane. Bob and Jane have two children each from prior marriages. They came into the marriage with about equal amounts in assets. They set up a Survivor's Trust/QTIP Trust plan to help protect the first to die's beneficiaries from later being changed by the surviving spouse. Bob passed away first leaving Jane a widow in her 70s. After a few years, Jane has met a new man, and they get married. Jane wishes to leave her trust assets to her new husband. She can do this with regard to her Survivor's Trust assets but not for the QTIP Trust assets as those are Bob's assets left for the benefit of Jane for the rest of her life. There are a few different ways to craft the QTIP Trust. One way is to give Jane access to all of the income and principal of the QTIP Trust. Another is for her to only have access to just the income. Jane can be the Trustee of the QTIP Trust if Bob and Jane had agreed to that in the trust or a separate third party can be in charge of the QTIP Trust (or the third party can be a Co-Trustee with the surviving spouse after the death of the first spouse). The plan is quite flexible and can be crafted to match the intentions of the couple.

As of 2024, this plan is generally most appropriate for: (1) couples with a combined trust estate under $13,610,000 (or $7,000,000 after the 2026 anticipated law change); (2) those who do not anticipate a large growth in their joint estate value beyond $13,610,000 in the next two years; (3) couples with blended families; (4) those who would like creditor protection at the death of the first spouse for the surviving spouse; and (5) those who wish to protect the first to die's estate for the reminder beneficiaries (so that the beneficiaries of the QTIP Trust cannot be changed in the absence of a Limited Power of Appointment) given to the surviving spouse. However, there is one note of caution, the Federal Estate Tax Exemption is set to sunset at the end of 2025, and the recommendation for fitness of this type of plan may change and be most appropriate for combined estates valued less than $7,000,000 (also note that the death benefit of life insurance policies that you own are also included in the value of your estate for Federal Estate Tax purposes).

The Clayton Election:

Finally, we consider the Clayton election. This option provides more flexibility for A/B trust planning without all the limitations on capital gains tax treatment for Bypass trust assets when the surviving spouse later dies. With this strategy, the plan is designed as an A/B trust plan but allows an independent executor to elect QTIP treatment over the deceased spouse's assets by an election made on the decedent's 706 death tax return. The election may include up to the entire amount deceased spouse's share, but may also only be a portion of it.

Any property of the decedent for which the QTIP election is not made then funds to the Bypass trust. Assets in the QTIP trust would be includible in the surviving spouse's estate at death, receiving a step up in basis at that time. If the beneficiaries later sell assets that were inherited through the QTIP trust, the capital gains tax liability is typically much lower (often zero depending on when a sale is executed).

The Bypass trust and the QTIP trust can be drafted to be substantially the same. This way the spouse who dies first can ensure that the remainder beneficiaries of the trust are not later changed (subject to any testamentary power of appointment given to the surviving spouse in the trust document). Keep in mind that the QTIP and Bypass trusts are "marital" trusts for the benefit of the surviving spouse and become "irrevocable" when the first spouse passes.

If there is a long-standing marriage with joint children, the couple may want to give the surviving spouse a "testamentary" limited power of appointment to reallocate the assets of the QTIP or Bypass trusts among their descendants, charities, and/or spouses of descendants. But in a blended family, the couple may not want this provision because the surviving spouse could reallocate the Bypass or QTIP trust assets if given this provision, disinheriting the deceased spouse's children or other beneficiaries.

Another advantage of the Clayton approach is that the election is made by an independent executor to avoid potential gift tax exposure by the surviving spouse. It also provides more objectivity in considering the benefits and drawbacks, especially in a blended family. Your CPA or attorney could be given the power to make the election.

Because the Clayton election is made on a timely filed 706 death tax return, the decision to send assets to the QTIP trust must be made within 9 months of the death of the first spouse to die. (A 6-month extension may be obtained, extending the time to make the election up to 15 months after the death of the first spouse.)

There is an added cost to have a 706 prepared after the death of the first spouse, but on the whole, there are great advantages to the Clayton election especially in a moderate to larger estate. These include asset protection for the deceased spouse's share, continuity of the remainder beneficiaries and an additional basis adjustment for assets in the QTIP trust after the surviving spouse later dies. It also allows for a wait and see approach to determine which of the two marital trusts to fund will likely produce a better tax result or if both should be funded for the best results.

Because the Clayton election is made on the 706, this provides the additional opportunity to claim portability of the deceased spouse's Unused Exemption Amount for any unused exemption of the decedent.

The surviving spouse's Survivor's trust property and the property in the QTIP trust are both included in the survivor's estate. Those assets receive a second step-up in basis when the surviving spouse later dies. But the survivor may also leverage the deceased spouse's ported estate tax exemption in case it's later necessary to use it. The survivor enjoys asset protection for the QTIP trust assets, and a "reverse QTIP election" can also leverage the deceased spouse's GST tax exemption. (This is important because the deceased spouse's estate tax exclusion is portable on a 706, but the GST exclusion is not.)

Flexibility is the key to the Clayton election's power. For smaller and medium-sized estates, we won't know the best course of action until the death of the first spouse to die. We may want to place assets that are rapidly appreciating into a QTIP trust so we secure a step-up in basis and avoid capital gains tax upon the death of the surviving spouse. Other clients may opt for the stronger asset protection features of a Bypass trust, especially if capital gains exposure is not a major factor when funding the plan after the death of the first spouse.

It is important to note that not utilizing a Bypass trust and using portability instead to preserve a first spouse's exemption has some flaws. The DSUEA does not adjust for inflation, and it is lost upon remarriage of the surviving spouse. Using a Bypass trust may make more sense to preserve the use of the DSUEA in some estates.

Protection for children in a prior marriage situation is arguably superior with a Bypass trust as well since we would not be at risk of an independent executor failing to make the QTIP election. Allocation of the deceased spouse's GST exemption to a Bypass can be more easily accomplished as well. One other note to make about QTIP and Bypass trusts is important to make here. Selection of who the Trustee will be of those marital trusts is important. The surviving spouse <u>can</u> be the Trustee, but if they are given distribution access to income and principal, those trusts could be depleted over the surviving spouse's lifetime. The surviving spouse, surviving spouse with a designated co-Trustee, or a separate independent Trustee can all be designated choices in advance.

So Which Approach Is "Best"?

There are several "soft" issues to consider when recommending a plan to a client. These issues include the desire to provide asset protection for the surviving spouse and to preserve who the jointly chosen remainder beneficiaries are after the death of the first spouse.

As counselors we are often asked which plan the client should choose. Unfortunately, the answer is not always clear cut. We must dig deep with clients to assess not only the transfer tax ramifications, but the income tax and family harmony implications as well. We must also explore the couple's tolerance for risk associated with allowing the survivor to change the plan after the first spouse's death. This issue becomes even more complex when there is a blended marriage in which one or both of the spouses have children from a prior marriage.

eight

Creditor Protection for Your Child's Inheritance

When leaving property to a minor or adult child, clients can choose exactly how they want to leave it to them. The property can be left outright, in trust until the beneficiary reaches a certain age or achieves a certain goal in life or in a continuing trust for that child's lifetime. For the last option, there is a special technique that allows us to help protect the money in a continuing trust for that child for his or her lifetime with maximum creditor protection. I have done this in my own trust to protect my children and we always discuss this option with our clients.

To protect your children in your trust using the continuing trust option, there are two basic requirements. The first is to have "no demand right" by your child against the Trustee as to the assets in their trust and the second is who you select as the Trustee (Interested vs. Independent Trustee).

To address the first consideration, what does it mean to have "no demand right"? Does the trust have language that allows the beneficiary to "demand" money from the Trustee?

Another common term used to explain this is the beneficiary's "withdrawal right." An example might be that Johnny has the right to withdraw up to 25% of the principal and income from his trust when he reaches the age of 25 and may exercise an unlimited withdrawal right when he reaches 30 for the entire trust balance. Although this might seem like a perfectly fine thing to draft for Johnny, having this type of demand right allows a future creditor to potentially tap into Johnny's trust for up to the percentage that he has a demand right for. Some examples of future creditors include a divorcing spouse, a bankruptcy trustee, a plaintiff in a lawsuit, or a business creditor. Whatever Johnny has a demand right over, so too might his future creditor in court.

Here is where it gets interesting. There are two types of Trustees: (1) the "interested" Trustee and (2) the "discretionary" Trustee. Under IRC 672(c), an interested Trustee is a related or subordinate party to the beneficiary or trust Grantor. Someone that is a first degree relative is a related party (so think, parent, sibling or child of the beneficiary or trust Grantor). By subordinate we mean someone working directly for the beneficiary or Trust Grantor. One note, a beneficiary's CPA or attorney is not considered a subordinate under the Code and therefore is **not** considered an Interested Trustee in this context.

For the best protection, we want a "discretionary" (or independent) Trustee making trust distributions if there is ever a real creditor threat. This is because a discretionary Trustee may make distributions for <u>any</u> purpose and may refuse to make distributions to the beneficiary for <u>any</u> reason. So, if the beneficiary was being sued and plaintiff's counsel was seeking money from the beneficiary's trust, a discretionary Trustee (Independent Trustee) can decide not to make a distribution to pay the judgment. That discretionary Trustee could also use his or her discretionary status as a bargaining chip to help settle a claim for a lesser amount on behalf of the beneficiary.

This is because a discretionary trustee may make distributions for any purpose and may refuse to make distributions to the beneficiary for any reason.

On the other hand, although there can be some limited protection with an interested Trustee who is limited to the HEMS Standard (Health, Education, Maintenance or Support), there are some holes. One such hole could be a divorcing spouse of the beneficiary. Because an interested Trustee must make HEMS standard distributions to the beneficiary, a divorcing spouse might be able to argue and successfully force an interested Trustee to distribute for alimony or child support.

Even if a client wants to list an interested party to serve as Trustee, we can still provide more protection by listing a discretionary Trustee in succession after the interested Trustee or by allowing the interested Trustee to resign and appoint an independent discretionary Trustee as his or her successor. That way if a creditor, predator, or divorcing spouse claim were a potential threat, the interested Trustee could resign and the discretionary Trustee could be appointed. There has been debate among practitioners as to how far removed from the Grantor or beneficiary that the independent Trustee should be to provide the best creditor protection. I believe it is a continuum of protection. For example, not many could argue the true discretionary nature of a bank or Trust Company Trustee. Now, on the other hand, although a cousin might be a discretionary Trustee, there is probably an argument that can be made that that type of discretionary Trustee is not as far removed and might be subject to some influence by a beneficiary regarding distributions from the trust.

Regardless, there is a distinct advantage to having any discretionary Trustee serve over an interested Trustee. The beneficiary can use it as a bargaining chip in negotiations with a creditor. But, the Grantor can provide some creditor protection for their children, but not rule from the grave by allowing the child of a separate share trust to act as sole Trustee (and/or as co-Trustee) of his or her own trust at a stated age of maturity. Then, later on down the road, if a potential creditor threat arises, the beneficiary Trustee (who is considered an interested Trustee) could resign and a discretionary Trustee already named, or then nominated, could take over as Trustee. In the alternative, the Grantor could give the beneficiary the right to choose his or her own successor discretionary Trustee.

If no issue ever arose in the future, the beneficiary Trustee would simply continue to remain in the driver's seat as Trustee. If upon death there are still assets inside the continuing trust, there can be provisions in the trust that shift that money to the next generation (or to anyone, really) with the same protective trust provisions.

In the alternative, if the trust share were left outright to the beneficiary, he or she would likely not be able to attain the same level of protection, even with a DAPT (Domestic Asset Protection Trust – See Chapter Twelve) which is a self-settled irrevocable trust. For example, if the bulk of the beneficiary's assets are from an inheritance, the beneficiary is not likely going to be able to place all of the assets into a DAPT because this would make him or her insolvent (the courts frown upon this type of action). However, if that money is left in a protective continuing trust set up by a parent (which is a third-party trust), the entire amount can remain protected. This is pretty powerful stuff.

nine

Nominating a Guardian for a Minor Child

If you have minor children, it is highly advised that you create a Guardianship Nomination designating who you wish to have physical custody of your children in the event of your incapacity or death (assuming your child's other parent is also incapacitated, deceased or their parental rights have been terminated). The importance of the stand-alone Guardianship Nomination is two-fold. First, it gives the court guidance on who you want to take custody of your children both temporarily and permanently. Secondly, it prevents your other estate planning documents from being lodged with the court (i.e., your will) and preserves the privacy of your estate.

A well-crafted Guardianship Nomination will nominate both temporary and permanent guardians for your children. This is critical, especially in situations where your designated permanent guardians live out of the area. No one wants Child Protective Services to have to take their children into custody, even if it were just temporarily. The Guardianship Nomination can also contain your wishes that your children be raised together, they be raised in your home if possible, and that both sides of your family maintain a relationship with your children.

13 Tips for Choosing a Guardian for Your Minor Child

While it's difficult enough to think about not being there to raise your children, imagine a court choosing a guardian with no input from you. Imagine your relatives arguing in court over who gets your children—or having them agree on someone you would not have chosen. That's why it's important to nominate a guardian while it's still up to you. Here are some tips to help you make your best choice.

Tip #1: Think beyond the obvious choices. Make a list of all the people you know who you would trust to take care of your children. You don't need to limit your list to close family members. While siblings and parents can be excellent choices, consider also extended family members who are old enough to raise your children – cousins, aunts, uncles, nieces, nephews, even second cousins once removed.

Tip #2: Friends can make excellent guardians. Beyond family, consider close friends, families with whom your family is close, the families of your children's friends, friends you know from your place of worship, even teachers or childcare providers with whom you and your children have a special relationship.

Tip #3: Don't stress about finances or the size of someone's house. Don't eliminate anyone from consideration because you don't think they have the financial wherewithal to take care of your children. You can take care of the finances with what you leave them or by having adequate life insurance. You can even instruct your trustee to provide funds for your chosen guardian to build an addition to their home or move to a larger home to accommodate your children.

A well-crafted Guardianship Nomination will nominate both temporary and permanent guardians for your children.

Tip #4: Focus on love. Consider whether each couple or person on your list would truly love your children if appointed their guardian. If they have children of their own, will your children play second fiddle? Or is the couple sufficiently loving to make your children feel loved no matter what?

Tip #5: Consider values and philosophies. Ask yourself which people on your list most closely share your values and philosophies with respect to your morals and religious beliefs, child-rearing, education, and social values.

Tip #6: Personality counts. Consider whether each of your candidates has the personality traits that would work for your children. Are they loving? Are they good role models? Do they have the patience to take on parenting your children? How affectionate are they? (If your family is particularly affectionate, a guardian who is loving but not physically affectionate could be damaging.) If they're fairly young, how mature are they?

Tip #7: Consider practical factors. For example: How would raising children fit into their lifestyle? If they're older, do they have the necessary health and stamina? Do they really want to be parents of a young child at their stage in life? Do they have other children? How would your children get along with theirs? Are there potential problems if your children were to live with theirs? How easily could the problems be dealt with? (For instance, do you want to place a child who struggles in school with a high-achieving child of the same age for whom everything comes easily?).

How close do they live to other important people in your children's lives? If a couple divorced, or one person died, would you be comfortable with either of them acting as the sole guardian?

Tip #8: Look for a good – but not a perfect – choice. Most likely, no one on your list will seem perfect – that is, just like you. But if you truly consider what matters to you most, you will probably be able to make some reasonable choices. In the end, trust your instincts. If one couple or person meets all of your criteria, but for some reason doesn't feel right, don't choose them. By the same token, if someone feels much more right than any of the others on your list, there's good reason for it. Make your primary choice, then some backup choices. It's essential that both you and your spouse agree. If you cannot decide, or if you and your spouse cannot agree, a good counseling-based estate-planning attorney can help you through the process.

Tip #9: Select a temporary as well as a permanent guardian. Temporary guardians may be appointed if both parents become temporarily unable to care for their children – for example, as the result of a car accident. Depending on your choice for permanent guardians, you may want to designate different people to act as temporary guardians. If your choice for a permanent guardian lives a considerable distance away, choose someone close by to serve as temporary guardian. If you're temporarily disabled, you'll want your children close by, and you won't want their lives unnecessarily disrupted by moving them to a new town and school. If you have no relatives or close friends nearby, consider the families of your children's friends. It's also important to have temporary guardians in your area because it may take time for your permanent guardians to arrive.

Tip #10: Consider a Guardianship Panel. Because it's difficult to predict what your children's needs will be as they grow older, consider appointing a "Guardianship Panel" to decide who would be the best guardian when and if it becomes necessary. Choose trusted relatives and friends to make up the panel. This allows for maximum flexibility, so the most appropriate choice can be made at the time a guardian is needed. The Panel can consult with your children and assess their needs and desires to make the most appropriate choice based on the current situation.

Tip #11: Write down your reasons. If you've chosen friends over relatives, or a more distant relative over a closer one, be sure to explain your decision in writing. That way – in the unlikely event your choice is challenged by people who feel they should have been chosen – a court should readily uphold your decision, knowing you've made your choice for good, solid reasons.

Tip #12: Have backup guardians. Nominate at least 3 guardians in successive order. If a first-choice guardian is unable or unwilling to take custody of your children, the Court will know your second and third choices for raising your children.

Tip #13: Talk with everyone involved. If your children are old enough and mature enough, talk with them to get their input as well. And be sure to confer with the people you'd like to choose, to ensure they're willing to be chosen and would feel comfortable acting as guardians. Once you've made your choice, there are steps you can take to make sure the potential guardians you've chosen will have the guidance and support they need. Here are a few ideas:

Draft a letter to convey information about your children, your parenting values and your hopes and dreams for your children. Set up a trust that will hold the assets you pass to your children and instruct the Trustee to provide necessary financial assistance to the guardians. You can also create specific instructions in a letter about special things you'd like the trust funds used for (for example, annual trips for your children to visit close friends and relatives, a particular summer camp, etc.). Designate "mentors" as special people in your children's lives to help guide them in ways for which the "mentor" is particularly well suited.

For instance, the person you choose for Trustee may also be a good "financial" mentor for your children. Or you may want to designate a "spiritual" mentor, particularly if the guardians you choose have religious philosophies that differ from yours. You can also name in your estate planning documents people who you simply want to have ongoing involvement in your children's lives. This can be a good way to include both sides of the family.

ten

Stretching Out and Protecting Your Retirement Accounts for Your Children with a Retirement Protector Trust™

What Is a Retirement Protector Trust?

A Retirement Protector Trust is a trust that acts as a shield or barrier to insulate the principal of your IRA, 401(k) or other retirement account from the trust beneficiary's creditors, a bankruptcy, a lawsuit, or a divorcing spouse after they inherit the accounts from you. This is accomplished by having the Retirement Protector Trust itself as the primary or contingent beneficiary of your retirement account(s).

Benefits of a Retirement Protector Trust

Having a stand-alone trust for your retirement accounts is advantageous because some of the provisions in your regular revocable trust may interrupt your successor Trustee's ability to creditor protect the retirement account for your beneficiaries. For example, the payment of funeral expenses, taxes and other final expenses upon your death can be problematic for any stretch-out based on developing case law in some jurisdictions. In a stand-alone Retirement

Protector Trust, these provisions are not included to avoid any potential issue on that front in the future.

Just to be clear, the trust never becomes the owner of your retirement account. It is simply the receptacle (the beneficiary) of any distributions from your retirement account. Who you select as your Trustee and the provisions drafted in the trust for each beneficiary will govern what happens when and whether there is creditor protection for your child or other beneficiary. The Retirement Protector Trust is a specialty trust in estate planning which not all practitioners are versed in drafting due to its complexity.

Should I Make the Trust "Beneficiary Controlled?"

Some may wish to give their children the opportunity to manage the trust as a beneficiary-controlled trust at some point in the future (e.g., at the age of 30 or older). This allows the child more substantial control over when and for what purposes funds are withdrawn. There is no right or wrong way to draft the trust, but there are preferred methods. Your particular situation, your thoughts and feelings on this topic, and sound advice from a skilled and competent estate planning attorney will govern how the trust should ultimately be crafted.

A note of caution: If you do make the trust beneficiary-controlled at a specified age, you do increase liability exposure. Accordingly, if your child experiences a bankruptcy or other creditor issue, he or she should resign as Trustee immediately and replace himself or herself with a third-party Independent

Trustee or request the Trust Protector to do so (which is actually a more conservative approach).

Another unique benefit of the Retirement Protector Trust is that you may list several beneficiaries. Each may also have distinct trust provisions. This may become important, especially if the beneficiary is afflicted with a drug or alcohol problem, is a minor or has poor spending habits. If the beneficiary has special needs issues, their share of the retirement account should flow through a retirement protector trust with the special needs person as the only beneficiary.

Establishing the Trust

Let's look at how the trust works in a practical sense. If you are married, you will want to set up a stand-alone Retirement Protector Trust for you and one for your spouse. This is the recommended approach due to the complexity of the IRA rules that determine who the accounts will go to in the future. It's also unknown who will pass first. For most couples, after you and your spouse are both gone, your retirement accounts will designate your Retirement Protector Trust as the contingent beneficiary of the account. The Trustee of your trust will have an opportunity to stretch out the account on behalf of your children if they are minors. In most cases, if they are not minors, all the funds must be withdrawn from your retirement accounts and added to the trust within ten years.

If your beneficiary form lists your Retirement Protector Trust with separate accounts for each trust beneficiary, the

Trustee can separate the account into separate shares. A qualified attorney can help prepare the beneficiary form for you to ensure this key step is properly done or provide details on how to do so.

Using an Accumulation Style Retirement Trust

By way of example, if you have two children as the beneficiaries of an accumulation style Retirement Protector Trust who inherit at the ages of 50 and 55, and your IRA has a $1 million balance, each child's share must be distributed to your Retirement Protector Trust within ten (10) years following your death. Distributions to the trust are made time over the ten year period but must be completed by the end of year on the 10th year per the Secure Act 2.0.

Using a "Conduit" Trust for Minors

If the trust is drafted as a Conduit Trust because your children are minors, the Trustee pays out an RMD (Required Minimum Distribution) directly to your child's guardian or through the trust. Each child reports the distribution to the IRS on an individual 1040 income tax return for that year.

Who Should Use a Retirement Protector Trust?

Retirement Protector Trusts are ideal for individuals with large retirement accounts ($300,000 plus) who want to protect their accounts for their children or grandchildren and create a creditor shield around the account(s) for those who inherit them.

Accumulation Style Example:

John, 57, and Sandy, 56, have been married for 25 years. They have two young adult children: Max, who is 22, and Alexis, who is 24. John was the breadwinner in the family while Sandy took care of the kids at home, so all of the retirement accounts are in his name. John retired early since his company got purchased, and he experienced the windfall of that transaction. John's IRA has about $800,000 in it. Although their children are great kids, with Alexis having graduated from college and Max finishing up college, they are still young and inexperienced. John and Sandy want to ensure that the kids don't make poor decisions with the money they will eventually inherit by creating accumulation style Retirement Protector Trusts and they want to protect the inheritance from any future spouses of Max and Alexis.

John and Sandy each set up a Retirement Protector Trust. Each of their trusts is a revocable trust funded with an arbitrary $10 during their lifetimes. John has updated his beneficiary form for his IRA to list Sandy as the primary beneficiary and his Retirement Protector Trust as the contingent beneficiary.

In John and Sandy's Retirement Protector Trusts they are each their own current Trustee, respectively, while they are alive. After they are both gone their designated Successor Trustee will administer the trusts until each of their children has reached the age of 35. When a child reaches the age of 35, each child's separate share trust becomes "beneficiary-controlled" meaning that the child can control his or her sub-trust as Trustee.

Each child at that age can act as their own Trustee and will need to ensure that 100% of each retirement account has been withdrawn from the retirement accounts and distributed to their share of the retirement protector trust. John and Sandy want to give their children flexibility and control, but not until they are much more mature and more likely to make wise choices. After their children take over as trustees at 35, (after John and Sandy have passed) they can each make distributions to themselves or allow the money in the trust to "accumulate."

Special provisions in the accumulation trust allow the income distributed from the retirement account to the trust to be income taxed at the beneficiary's income tax rate instead of the trust income tax rate which is typically higher. This creates an income tax advantage while allowing the income to be protected in the trust without forcing a distribution to the beneficiary.

If even greater creditor protection for a beneficiary from a divorcing spouse, creditor, predator or bankruptcy is desired, an independent Trustee not related or subordinate to the Grantor or beneficiary should be selected to manage the trust and make distributions, or the child beneficiary could be given the power to later resign and appoint an independent Trustee.

Lastly, a Trust Protector (an independent 3rd-party that can limitedly amend the trust if changes to the law occur, a new trustee is needed due to a vacancy, etc.) should be included in the trust for maximum flexibility for the future.

eleven

Why LLCs Make for Great Asset Protection for Your Rental Real Estate

The basic idea behind asset protection planning for real estate (other than the family home) is to create a legal separation between you and the real estate. This can be accomplished with a Limited Liability Company (LLC). LLCs can also be great vehicles for privacy and for tax and estate planning. The more properties you acquire, the more likely you are to become the party to a lawsuit on one or more of the properties. Putting an asset protection barrier between you and your real estate should be a top priority as soon as you acquire any commercial or residential rental real estate.

There are a variety of ways in which a property owner can lose their hard-earned assets to even just one successful lawsuit. Some typical causes are injured tenants, delivery people, guests on the property, neighbors, criminals, children wandering on to the property and getting hurt, or even a city repairman. All it takes is one devastating event, and you could be wiped out.

Putting an asset protection barrier between you and your real estate should be a top priority

A person on the property could slip and fall or a balcony could collapse. Not to mention that buildings do catch on fire and mold can grow in the strangest places and cause extreme damage not just to the property itself but to its inhabitants. You can be sued not just for things you are aware of but also for things you "should have" been aware of. A court could decide that you should have known to repair the property to prevent the harm that resulted.

It is not uncommon for a new client to come into my office owning real estate either outright in their name or in the name of their revocable trust. The problem is that if they are successfully sued, the whole of their assets are subject to satisfy that claim or judgment. So, when I see a situation like this, I immediately ask about their insurance liability coverage on the properties, whether they have an umbrella policy, and if they know they should set up a Limited Liability Company (LLC) to shield their other assets from a future claim.

Ideally, for the best asset protection, you want to place each rental or commercial property in its own separate LLC. The reason is that if a claim arises on one property, it will not take them all down. If they are all in the same LLC and a major judgment against the LLC occurs, all of the assets of the LLC

SECRETS OF GREAT ESTATE PLANNING

could be subject to satisfy the judgment. This however is a matter of law which will depend upon the jurisdiction under which you form your LLC. Some states have stronger LLC statutes that better protect the owners of the LLC.

For example, some state statutes limit the creditor's remedy to a charging order. A charging order limits the creditor to the LLC member's share of distributions, without conferring on the creditor any voting or management rights in the LLC. If the member decides not to make any distributions, then the creditor would not get any either.

After the LLC is properly set up, you will want to change the title to the property to the name of the LLC. Although some lenders on commercial and residential rental property may have "due on sale" clauses buried in their mortgage documents, most rarely exercise them. Most banks are very familiar with the reasons people want to hold title in the name of an LLC and a simple call to the lender can clear up any questions. The bank will likely want to make sure that the LLC is owned by the same parties that are the parties to the loan on the property.

When the deed to transfer the title to the LLC is prepared, you will also need to file a proportional interest statement and a preliminary change of ownership report so you don't trigger an Assessor's Office transfer tax or reassessment. (and provide them with a copy of the LLC operating agreement). After the transfer is recorded at the Recorder's Office, you will want to assign your right, title, and interest in the LLC to your revocable trust so it doesn't later trigger a probate. If you are in need of estate tax reduction strategies, you may even want to set up an Intentionally Defective Grantor Trust and transfer a portion of the LLC to that legal entity. However, that is a very complex discussion and goes beyond the scope of this chapter. Consult legal counsel before taking on this type of planning for taxes.

Once the property is moved into the LLC, your other assets will be shielded from future lawsuits arising from the property so long as you respect the existence of the entity and keep it in good standing. Only the assets of the LLC could be at risk to satisfy the lawsuit. An LLC formed in California must file a Statement of Information every 2 years and pay an annual Franchise Tax Board (most often, the fee is $800 per year but could be higher if gross receipts are in excess of $250,000).

Without Asset Protection Planning

Here's an example of what happened to a couple who are real estate investors and did not do asset protection planning:

Bill and Cindy own two residential rental properties in San Diego. The rentals are owned individually in their names as joint tenants. One of the properties as it turned out had some bad wiring and caused a fire in the home. A tenant was killed in the blaze. The surviving spouse of the tenant sued Bill and Cindy in their individual names and was awarded a judgment of $2.8 million. Bill and Cindy have a $1 million liability policy on the property and the insurance company paid that amount to the surviving spouse of the deceased tenant. There was still $1,800,000 outstanding on the judgment. The surviving spouse started collections proceedings against Bill and Cindy to take their personal residence and all their bank accounts, the other rental property, and their investment accounts. The only thing left untouched was their 401Ks. In a nutshell, they are financially devastated.

With Proper Asset Protection Planning

By contrast, let's look at an example where two real estate investors invested in proper asset protection planning:

Tom and Bob own two rental properties together. Originally, they purchased them as joint tenants. However, Tom's attorney told Tom that he recommended that the properties be held in an LLC so that Tom's other assets would not be at risk if a lawsuit was ever filed in relation to the properties. Tom's attorney also recommended that he assign his interest in the LLC to his revocable trust so that his half goes to his family if he died.

Tom and Bob decided to set up two LLCs since they own two properties. They liked the idea that if something bad happened to one of the properties, it would not affect the other property, and they liked the idea of protecting their other assets.

A heavy storm came through late in January and resulted in the roof collapsing in one of the properties. One of the tenants was killed when the roof collapsed. Tom and Bob didn't know of any problems with the roof, but the court ruled that they should have known that the roof would likely collapse in heavy rain and wind conditions. The judgment was for $1.7 million, however, the plaintiffs settled for $1 million because their attorney counseled them that they were limited in recovery to the insurance policy limit and the equity in the LLC.

The property and casualty insurance policy paid the first $100,000 and the umbrella insurance policy paid the next $900,000. Tom and Bob only had $100,000 in equity in the home, but because the home was destroyed in the storm, that equity is gone. Because Tom and Bob properly formed their LLC, put this home in its own separate LLC, and properly maintained the LLC, the plaintiff cannot get to Tom and Bob's other assets outside the LLC.

twelve

Protecting Part of Your Net Worth with a Domestic Asset Protection Trust

Just what is a Domestic Asset Protection Trust, or what is more commonly referred to as a DAPT? It's a type of irrevocable trust that is self-settled and acts like a spendthrift trust which doesn't allow for the appointment of the trust assets to your creditors and permits you to be a beneficiary. In plain English, it's a trust you can set up in certain states to protect assets from your future creditors and lawsuits against you. In a DAPT, there is an "independent" Trustee who has discretionary power to make (or not make) distributions to the beneficiaries of the trust. The Grantor of the DAPT is usually a beneficiary of the trust.

The Domestic Asset Protection Trust got its start in 1997 when Alaska enacted its statute allowing for self-settled asset protection trusts. Since then, many other states have enacted similar asset protection statutes. However, not all of these state statutes provide the same level of protection to those seeking this type of creditor protection.

Of the present DAPT states, California is not one of them. However, that doesn't mean that you can't set one up in another state that allows them.

The Grantor of a DAPT can utilize the laws of a state that recognizes the DAPT even though the Grantor lives in another state that doesn't recognize self-settled asset protection trusts. In such cases, careful drafting, selection of an independent Trustee who resides in the DAPT state, and delivery of the trust assets to the independent Trustee are key. The type of asset transferred to the trust can also affect the analysis. For instance, the transfer of real estate from the Grantor's non-DAPT home state can be problematic. This necessarily could lead to a conflict of laws because the Grantor's home state will likely exercise jurisdiction over the real property even if it's titled in the name of a DAPT.

On the flip side, an interesting benefit of the DAPT is that the Grantor can continue to pay the income taxes on the trust assets, allowing him or her to further "burn" or deplete his or her taxable estate if the trust is properly drafted. In some cases, there may be an opportunity to save income taxes as well.

The states with DAPT statutes are Alaska, South Dakota, Delaware, Nevada, Utah, Alabama, Connecticut, Indiana, Ohio, Tennessee, Wyoming, Rhode Island, New Hampshire, Missouri, Hawaii, Virginia, West Virginia, Oklahoma, Michigan, Mississippi, and Colorado. The fact that there are now twenty-on states allowing for self-settled asset protection trusts shows that this strategy is becoming more widely accepted.

Though each state statute varies, they all have certain common characteristics and must meet the following criteria as a DAPT: (1) the trust must be irrevocable; (2) the trust must be a "spendthrift" type trust; (3) there must be at least one Trustee of the trust who is a resident in the state in which the DAPT was formed; (4) at least some of the administration of the DAPT must happen in the state the DAPT was formed; and (5) the Grantor (Settlor) of the DAPT should not act as a Trustee.

There are some attractive powers that can be retained by the Grantor of the trust under some of the DAPT state statutes. Some states allow a Grantor to veto distributions, appoint investment advisors, appoint trust protectors, and even to direct trust investments. Some states even allow the Grantor to remove and replace the Trustee. Some states have gone even farther and allow the Grantor to move the domicile of the trust to an offshore jurisdiction. In such states, the Trustee may remove the asset protection trust and its assets outside the U.S.

Although this asset protection device has been around for a decade and a half, it has generally not been seen in the Court system except in the case of a bankruptcy. Most cases settle out of court for some lesser negotiated amount due to the expense in litigating to get to the assets. Other than in the case of a bankruptcy, DAPTs have proven to be quite effective bargaining chips for settling for a lesser amount and protecting the trust assets from the reach of creditors and lawsuits.

There are various state statutes for DAPTs across the country that govern how the trust needs to be set up and how and from whom the assets can be protected. Most DAPT state statutes allow the DAPT to be a "Grantor" trust. This means among other things that the Grantor of the trust can pay the income tax on the income that the trust generates even though the trust is an irrevocable trust. Many types of assets can be transferred to a DAPT including cash, securities, real estate, and business interests, just to name a few.

In some DAPT jurisdictions, a new Affidavit of Solvency is required when new asset transfers are made to the trust. The states that do not require a new Affidavit of Solvency are Nevada, South Dakota, Delaware, Rhode Island, New Hampshire, Missouri, Hawaii, Virginia, Oklahoma, and Colorado. Although it may be good practice to file one even if not required.

Each state has a period of time that must vest before the assets are protected from a creditor's claim. This statute of limitations varies from state to state between one and a half to four years. The state with the lowest waiting period is Ohio at one and a half years. Nevada, South Dakota, Alaska, Tennessee,

Utah, and Hawaii all have a two-year statutory period. This generally means that if there are no known creditors at the time of the asset transfer, the assets are protected in the trust when the given statutory period expires.

Even though case law has been scant on the ability of creditors to pierce through a DAPT to reach the trust assets, there are some theories on how a creditor could pierce. The main one is the choice of law argument. A creditor could argue that the laws of the Grantor's home state (if the Grantor lives in a non-DAPT state) should be applied to the trust and not the DAPT state's laws.

A second argument might be to try to classify the transfer to the trust as fraudulent. This can largely be overcome however by doing this type of planning far in advance of any creditor issues. As long as the Grantor has not made a transfer to the trust in an attempt to hinder, delay, or defraud a creditor, this argument can be rebutted.

A creditor could also try to make an arguement under the U.S. Constitution Full Faith and Credit Clause. This clause holds that the laws of one state must recognize judgments of another. A creditor could try to file first in the Grantor's home state and ask that the DAPT state honor the judgment. However, there is a lack of case law to this point. It seems to be the case that creditors have not wanted to spend litigation dollars to pierce through to get to the assets in a DAPT.

Additionally, a federal court could ignore the laws of a state where the Supremacy Clause of the U.S. Constitution was involved. In some instances, federal law trumps state law. In such a situation, the DAPT state statute may not protect the trust assets in federal court or where a federal administrative agency is involved.

Lastly, the new bankruptcy rules since 2005 give bankruptcy Trustees greater power to set aside certain types of transactions that affect creditors. The bankruptcy Trustee could reach back as far as ten years from the bankruptcy petition filing for assets transferred to a DAPT, where the Grantor is a beneficiary of the DAPT and where the transfer was made with the intent to hinder, delay, or defraud a creditor.

Even given the possible arguments stated above, the case law on this is practically non-existent. Much of this is just legal postulation. The only real case law we have has been in the area of bankruptcy. The fact remains that these trusts create a significant barrier to help protect assets and act as a bargaining chip to aid in settlement negotiations of a debt, lawsuit, or other creditor claim.

So just who is a good candidate for this type of planning? Future liability concerns doctors, lawyers, high risk professionals, accountants, officers in public companies, those who own real estate, and other people of high net worth. The best protection is to set this structure up far in advance of any creditor problem. This is because each state has a statutory waiting period until the assets are *protected*. The DAPT can serve as a future "rainy day" fund in the event all goes sideways in the world of the Grantor.

A DAPT might also be a viable substitute for a prenuptial agreement. Transferring assets to a DAPT before marriage could act as a protection lever from a new spouse under the statutes of a state such as Nevada. It's true that prenuptial agreements serve a purpose. However, there are many reasons why couples don't execute them and even more why judges and juries disregard them in a divorce.

Prenuptial agreements can be challenged and considered invalid if not properly drafted, if they're later considered unfair or both parties weren't adequately represented by separate counsel. An alternative to executing a pre-nup is to transfer some of one's net worth to a DAPT prior to marriage. If you choose a state that doesn't included the spouse as an exception creditor, this technique can serve to protect a portion of your assets from a later divorce.

Next, let's examine the timing of an asset transfer. You don't want to get caught in the snare of a fraudulent transfer. A fraudulent transfer is any transfer of property out of your name that appears to have been made with the intent to hinder, delay, or defraud a creditor. This is for known or "foreseeable" creditors. A court could consider the transfer to a DAPT fraudulent if you transferred property to the trust after the threat of a creditor action or lawsuit has been filed or been threatened to be filed. Each state has its own statutory waiting period from the date the asset is transferred to the DAPT and when the asset is protected from a creditor's claim. For example, Nevada's statutory waiting period is two years, which is among the fastest waiting periods among all of the DAPT states.

> *Future liability concerns doctors, lawyers, high risk professionals, accountants, officers in public companies, those who own real estate, and other people of high net worth.*

There is also a statute of limitations that differs depending upon whether the creditor is a preexisting creditor or a non-preexisting creditor. If there is a preexisting creditor, there is a tolling of the statute of limitations period in order to protect those creditors.

Today there is a definite increase in liability exposure. We live in a victim mentality world where the revelation that someone has deep pockets can spur on a lawsuit or a threat of one. The plaintiffs' attorneys are partly to blame in this regard as well with their TV commercials making it appear to be the norm to sue sue sue! Many professionals are fearful of malpractice lawsuits today because of the notoriety of malpractice legal actions. For instance, in 2006, there were over 633,000 malpractice claims against physicians and surgeons alone! This was reported by the Physician Insurers Association, 2007 Report.

Nearly all of the states that allow for DAPTs also have exception creditor statutes. These statutes protect certain classes of creditors by allowing them access to a DAPT's assets. One common exception creditor is a divorcing spouse. There are two states that don't have exception creditors and they are Nevada and Utah.

Even though just implementing a Domestic Asset Protection Trust would stifle most would-be plaintiffs, there are additional asset protection strategies that can be utilized to significantly increase your asset protection if used in conjunction with the DAPT. By adding one or more Limited Liability Companies (LLCs) to the mix, you can limit a creditor's remedy to a "charging order" in some jurisdictions. A charging order limits the creditor to the LLC member's share of distributions and doesn't confer any voting or management rights to the creditor in the LLC. This charging order protection offers an additional barrier when it is combined with the DAPT in a well-crafted asset protection plan.

One final note on DAPTs. You also cannot make yourself insolvent by transferring all or most of your assets to a DAPT. The Court will want to see that you have some means of supporting yourself on assests or income outside of the DAPT.

thirteen

Planning for the Long-Term Care of an Elderly Parent

Long-term care planning is the process of looking forward and deciding in advance how you will handle the care of an aging parent, how that care will be paid for and who will provide that care should a situation arise where mom or dad can no longer live independently. As we all age, the risk of needing long-term care grows. Afflictions such as Alzheimer's disease, dementia, strokes, heart attacks, and broken hips from falls are some of the most common reasons necessitating outside professional help or a nursing home stay.

Long-term care costs are rising at an alarming rate in California. It has become a major problem for most seniors. Many end up losing their life's savings, their homes, or both, paying for long term care. Statistics show that 60-70% of all seniors will need long term care at some point during their life. Studies show that the increased need for long-term care is due to the fact that the average life expectancy has risen so dramatically in recent years.

Long-term care costs are rising at an alarming rate in California.

The average cost per month for nursing home care statewide in California in 2023 was $10,390. However, the cost of long-term care is often much greater in larger counties such as Los Angeles, San Francisco, Orange and San Diego Counties, where the monthly cost of nursing home care can run as high as $13,000 or more depending upon the level of care needed.

If possible, it is wise to have a long-term care policy on board. But, in some cases, seniors are unable to qualify, and it may be impossible to get all of their medical needs met through traditional insurance. Therefore, Medi-Cal is the only option for ensuring coverage (or at least a part of the medical coverage) for a long-term care stay in a nursing facility.

To provide an example, imagine Aunt Betty who is 78. Aunt Betty often has lapses in her memory but all in all she is still able to take care of herself in her home. Aunt Betty has two adult children and several grandchildren but both of her children live out of state. Aunt Betty has a home in Southern California that is now worth close to $1,200,000 (she and her late husband purchased the home 40 years ago for $100,000). Betty also has a car but it's not in very good condition. She also receives social security income of $2,000/month and a small pension of $800/month from her late husband's company. Finally, she has a $100,000 CD at a local bank. Looking forward, there is a possibility that Betty may need in-home care or nursing care at a facility as a result of a dementia or an Alzheimer's disease diagnosis. Betty's mother developed Alzheimer's in her early 80's and lived with the disease for 10 years.

Can Betty be helped? There are strategies and techniques that can be used to plan in advance how Betty would like to be cared for and how the cost of care will be covered. By pre-planning, Aunt Betty may be able to preserve assets so that she does not end up in a crisis situation, requiring her to quickly spend down her estate. Aunt Betty also needs to make sure that she has an Advance Health Care Directive, HIPAA Authorization, Expanded Power of Attorney for Finances, as well as a trust to transfer assets to her children (or other beneficiaries if she so chooses).

It is probably also a good idea for Aunt Betty to consider a geriatric care manager to help her because her children live far away. Incapacity is not typically something that happens over night, but rather is a gradual process. Thus, in all circumstances, it is best to have someone there for an elder adult to rely on for support should he or she need more and more assistance down the road.

In Aunt Betty's case, her home is her largest asset. She really wants the home to be transferred to her children who grew up in the home. There are some important planning steps that should be undertaken to preserve the family home through a trust. Other assets may be transferred to her trust as we can also have a trusted person in charge of that trust as Trustee if the need were to arise where she could no longer manage her own finances and assets.

If a special type of irrevocable trust is used (aka Medicaid Asset Protection Trust) the sooner we do this, however, the better. California has adopted the DRA (Deficit Reduction Act of 2005) but has not yet implemented it. What this means is that there is currently a "look-back" period of 30 months in California. This means that gifts made 30 months before applying for long term care Medi-Cal could be subject to a transfer penalty without proper advance planning. Once the DRA is implemented in California, that rule will require applicants to provide Medi-Cal with 60 months of statements for all gifts made prior to applying and the penalty period doesn't start to run until the filing of the Medi-Cal application. New promulgated regulations have been introduced for public comment as of the publication date of this book. We are awaiting approval and adoption of the new rules, thereby changing California law.

Gifts made 30 months before applying for long term care Medi-Cal could be subject to a transfer penalty without proper advance planning.

One of the major changes that will occur under the DRA is when the penalty period will begin with respect to gifts being made. Currently, if any penalty period is triggered, the penalty runs from the date the gift was made, not when an application for benefits under Medi-Cal is submitted. That is expected to change when the DRA is implemented in California. The penalty period will run from the date of application for any gifts that trigger a penalty within a 60-month period prior to the date of application. This is a huge change from the current law and will severely restrict and affect new Medi-Cal applicants. This could impact many unknowing seniors who make gifts and who will need nursing home care in the near and distant future. It is uncertain if and when California will implement the DRA rules.

There are many other strategies and techniques to help aid a family in planning for long-term care. In some cases it may make sense for a senior to establish a revocable trust as part of the planning process for long term care. Careful planning is required when looking at the big picture. Additionally, other changes are anticipated in 2024 that could eliminate the assets test rule leaving only an income test for Medi-Cal benefits for long term nursing home coverage. Currently, assets transferred to a revocable trust avoid a Medicaid recovery action after the one who has received benefits has passed.

In the end, having a trust (either revocable or irrevocable) with the right provisions along with a Power of Attorney, Advance Health Care Directive, HIPAA, and other estate planning documents for an aging parent are key to helping to protect them, their assets, and keeping you and them out of the court system via a conservatorship during their lifetime during incapacity.

fourteen

What is Trust Administration and What Does a Successor Trustee Do?

When a loved one dies and they have a trust, the process of trust administration will need to be undertaken. Many lawyers make trust administration appear simple at the time their client signs the trust document without fully explaining what will need to happen after their death. This is dangerous because often the client never discusses trust administration with the designated Successor Trustee. The person or people that will serve as Trustee need to understand what should happen at the time of death of the person creating the trust.

Over the years, it has been our experience that clients sometimes have unrealistic expectations about how their trust will work when a death occurs. Clients sometimes think that the trust doesn't need any further attention and that everything will happen "automatically" or they don't realize that they will need the help of an attorney and CPA to administer the trust. These are common misconceptions. There are administrative duties and expenses that revolve around trust administration that families and Trustees need to understand.

One of the most frequent misunderstandings happens when there is a joint trust between a husband and a wife and the trust provisions call for the trust to be split into sub-trusts (most commonly between a Survivor's Trust and a Bypass Trust or QTIP Trust). The most common reasons for having this type of trust are estate tax savings, asset protection for the surviving spouse, and/or divorce-remarriage protection for the first to die's half of the estate.

What is key to remember is that by having a trust, the person or couple setting up the trust will avoid probate (provided the trust is properly funded before death) and there could be estate tax savings as a byproduct of the estate plan. Also, probate in California is expensive (often 5X more than the costs associated with trust administration), time consuming (typically 16-24 months on average), and open to the public's prying eyes.

...the person or couple setting up the trust will avoid probate...

The first thing that happens in a trust administration, if there is a call for a division of the trust or allocation into sub-trusts for beneficiaries, is that an "administrative" trust with its own tax identification number needs to be set up. This is for accounting purposes. The trust will likely need to pay for funeral and possibly last illness expenses of the deceased Grantor as well as bills and other administrative expenses like attorney and CPA fees. Typically, the successor Trustee will set up a new bank account in the name of the "administrative" trust to track all expenses.

There are many other things that can happen in a trust administration. Some of these things could include:

1.   Providing a legal Notice of the trust beneficiaries and heirs at law of the death of the Grantor;

2.   Obtaining an IRS Tax ID Number(s) for the trust (and sub-trusts, if any);

3.   Filing a final income tax return for the decedent;

4.   Filing a death tax return;

5.   Filing a trust income tax return annually for as long as the trust is held open;

6.   Publishing a legal notice in a local newspaper regarding the death of the Grantor of the trust (in some cases);

7.   Marshalling all of the assets together and protecting the trust assets;

8.   Opening a bank account for the trust;

9.   Paying financial and last expenses of the decedent;

10. Collecting life insurance policy proceeds;

11. Determining if a formal probate needs to be opened with the court for any assets not titled in the trust;

12. Notifying all banks and financial institutions of the death and that they are the nominated Successor Trustee;

13. Notifying the V.A. (if applicable) and Department of Healthcare Services of the death;

14. Determining beneficiary status of all the decedent's retirement accounts;

15. Obtaining valuations on all property as of the date of death of the decedent including real estate, brokerage accounts and business interests;

16. Determining if an estate tax is due on the decedent's Estate;

17. Paying off all of the debts of the Grantor of the trust from the assets of the trust;

18. Paying ongoing expenses of trust administration such as legal and CPA expenses, etc.;

19. Liquidating assets where necessary to pay off the debts of the Grantor;

20. Investing assets of the trust in a safe and prudent manner during trust administration;

21. Obtaining waivers of accounting and/or waivers of time to contest from all beneficiaries;

22. Obtaining signatures from all beneficiaries on a family settlement agreement;

23. Distributing the trust assets to the beneficiaries at the conclusion of the trust administration;

24. Providing a formal accounting to all beneficiaries where a waiver of accounting has not been signed by all beneficiaries;

25. Depositing the decedent's Will with the County Clerk for safe keeping;

26. Inform the Credit Bureau of the death to freeze the credit of the decedent;

27. Creating sub-trusts (if called for in the trust) for trust beneficiaries and funding those sub-trusts;

The above is not an exhaustive list. It is simply a list of common items a Trustee may be called to do. Also, it is important to note that each trust is unique and the situation and assets of the Grantor of that trust are unique. So, some things that may not occur in one trust administration may need to occur in another. Therefore, it is important to hire an experienced attorney for legal guidance. This can also help shield the successor Trustee from liability claims from the beneficiaries as well.

fifteen

Advanced Estate Planning Strategies

Annual Gifts to an Irrevocable Gifting Trust

If your estate exceeds the amount of the Federal Estate Tax exemption, one way to reduce the size of your estate and avoid estate taxes is to make gifts to your family members while you are still alive. As long as these gifts do not exceed the annual exclusion amount (in 2024, $18,000 per recipient per year), you will not have to file a gift tax return (IRS form 709) on the gifts. This means that you can give up to $18,000 to each of your children and/or grandchildren each year without any gift tax consequences.

An annual exclusion lifetime gifting program allows you to avoid gift, estate and generation-skipping transfer tax on transferred assets. Under the Internal Revenue Code, you can transfer up to $18,000 (2024) per year, per person, to anyone without incurring gift tax or the generation-skipping transfer tax. With a lifetime giving program, you can transfer this amount annually to the individuals of your choice, typically children, grandchildren, other close family members, or anyone really.

For example, if you give $18,000 per year to two beneficiaries for five years, you will have removed $180,000 from your estate for estate tax purposes. After 10 years, you will have removed more than $360,000 and nearly $900,000 after 25 years. We have many clients who would like to make annual gifts, but who don't want to lose control of the assets that they give away. For these clients, we recommend an Irrevocable Gifting Trust. These amounts can be doubled if you are married and gift split from community property funds.

one way to reduce the size of your estate and avoid estate taxes is to make gifts to your family members while you are still alive.

An Irrevocable Gifting Trust is a type of irrevocable trust that can provide complete asset protection for your children and/or grandchildren and it removes the trust assets from your estate and the estates of your children and/or grandchildren for estate tax purposes. This type of trust is very similar to a "Bypass" trust (one that bypasses the Federal Estate Tax) at death. If the trust is drafted as a spousal lifetime access trust, you don't lose access to the assets because your spouse can withdraw from the trust for health, education, maintenance or support.

Annual exclusion gifts can be used to shield transfers to an Irrevocable Gifting Trust from gift and generation-skipping transfer taxes. Each beneficiary must have the right to withdraw up to the amount of the transfer designated for that beneficiary or their pro rata of the gift, but if that right is not exercised, the gifted funds can then be used to purchase life insurance on the life of the transferor or for other investments. This trust can also be a multi-generational estate tax exempt trust or it can become a family "bank" for: (1) education; (2) business acquisitions; or (3) home purchases, among other things.

Intentionally Defective Grantor Trust (IDGT)

An IDGT or Intentionally Defective Grantor Trust is a type of irrevocable trust where the owner of property either gifts or sells the property to the trust to gain an estate tax advantage for their children or other beneficiaries down the road. The trust is drafted with any number of provisions that make the trust a "Grantor" trust for income tax purposes but allows transfers to the trust to be irrevocably transferred out of the Grantor's estate.

The reason the "Grantor" trust status is so desirable is because it allows the Grantor to pay the income taxes on the assets inside the IDGT at their individual income tax rate instead of trust tax rates and allows for a further "burn" of the Grantor's estate assets that are outside the trust. That is particularly important in larger estates because the payment by the Grantor of the income taxes on the IDGT assets is not considered a gift to the beneficiaries by the IRS. It's like a freebie we can get under the tax code in terms of transfers to the beneficiaries. This allows the assets in the IDGT to grow unencumbered by the income tax liability.

Another fringe benefit of the IDGT is the "freezing" of the value of the assets transferred to the IDGT to the value at the date of transfer. All future growth in the assets inside the IDGT grow free from the estate tax system and can pass to the beneficiaries without imposition of federal estate tax.

Lastly, where the assets transferred to the IDGT are business interests, there may be an opportunity to discount or "squeeze" the value of the property to lower than its current fair market value. For example, assume mom and dad own 50% of a closely held business with their interest worth a fair market value of $10MM. Mom and dad decide to gift 40% of their interest to an IDGT. With a proper valuation discount appraisal, the couple may be able to transfer $8MM of the business interest but only need to record a gift of $5,600,000 to the trust on a 709-gift tax return (for example, assuming a 30% business valuation discount). IDGTs are a popular and highly effective means to reduce or eliminate estate taxes with their "freeze", "squeeze" and "burn" properties to benefit current and future generations.

Irrevocable Life Insurance Trust
Life insurance is a unique asset because it serves numerous diverse functions in a tax-favored environment. Life insurance proceeds are income tax free and, if properly owned by an Irrevocable Life Insurance Trust, life insurance proceeds

can also be received free of estate tax. Some of the frequent uses for life insurance include:

a. **Wealth Creation**: Where age or other circumstances have prevented one from accumulating a desired level of wealth, life insurance can create instant wealth, for example, to build an estate, to care for dependents, to replace a key employee, to buy out the interest of a business co-owner at death, or to pay off a mortgage.

b. **Income Replacement**: Life insurance can provide wealth to replace income lost upon the premature death of the family "bread winner."

c. **Wealth Replacement**: Life insurance can provide the liquidity to pay estate or capital gain taxes after death. Life insurance can also be used to replace the value of gifts to charity or non-family members.

There are several types of life insurance, including term, permanent, and survivorship or second-to-die insurance. Term insurance, which includes annual renewable and fixed-level term, is temporary (for example, 20-year Level Term). At the end of the term, the policy terminates and the insured must reapply at the then-going rates, based upon age, health, etc.

or convert the policy at a higher premium rate, with some exceptions. Therefore, term insurance is often recommended for temporary needs. Permanent insurance, of which there are several types- whole life, universal life, and variable universal life are intended to remain in force until the insured's death, and thus are often recommended for permanent needs. Survivorship or second-to-die insurance pays out at the death of the surviving spouse. Therefore, second to die insurance is often recommended in those circumstances where the liquidity need arises only at the second death. For example, if there is a need for liquidity to pay estate taxes or to care for minor children.

Contrary to what many people think, at death, the death proceeds of life insurance you own are included in your estate for estate tax calculation purposes if the policy is owned by you. This adverse result can be avoided by transferring the life insurance policy to an Irrevocable Life Insurance Trust (or preferably having the trustee of the ILIT purchase a new policy on your life to avoid a three year look back rule) that would become the owner and beneficiary of the policy. The disposition terms of the trust can mirror the terms in your revocable living trust. Note that it is much more favorable to have the Irrevocable Life Insurance Trust purchase a new policy on your life as opposed to transferring an existing policy to the trust. This is due to the IRS three-year look back rule that could pull the insurance proceeds back into your estate if you die less than three years after the transfer of an "existing" policy to your Irrevocable Life Insurance Trust.

However, there are ways around this if you must use an existing policy.

A properly drafted Irrevocable Life Insurance Trust (ILIT) can accomplish the following objectives:

- Provide needed income for your spouse and children

- Prevent life insurance proceeds from being included in your taxable estate

- Provide your family with funds to pay estate tax and settlement expenses

- Provide the surviving spouse with access to the death benefit for his or her health, education, maintenance or support

- Protect the proceeds of the life insurance from your beneficiaries' creditors, predators, and divorcing spouses

- Care for your minor children and put them through college

- Provide for grandchildren

If you are concerned about accessing the cash value of the insurance during your lifetime, the trust can be carefully drafted so that the trustee can make loans to you during your lifetime or so that the trustee can make distributions to your spouse during your spouse's lifetime. Even with these provisions, the life insurance proceeds will not be included in your estate for estate tax purposes. You can create these trusts individually (which would own an individual policy on your life) or they can be created jointly by you and your spouse (with a survivorship life insurance policy).

The Qualified Personal Residence Trust

A Qualified Personal Residence Trust ("QPRT") is a type of trust specifically authorized by the Internal Revenue Code. It permits you to transfer ownership of your residence to your family during your lifetime and retain the exclusive right to live in the residence, while reducing the size of your estate for estate tax purposes.

The residence is transferred to the Qualified Personal Residence Trust for a designated initial term of years. Provided you survive the initial term of years, ownership of the residence will be transferred to your family at a fraction of its fair market value. If you die during the initial term of years, the property will be brought back into your estate, but you will be no worse off than had you not created the Qualified Personal Residence Trust. You may transfer up to three (3) personal residences into Qualified Personal Residence Trusts (your primary residence and two vacation homes if you are married).

The Qualified Personal Residence Trust is a particularly noteworthy estate planning tool to reduce Federal Estate Taxes. It permits you to transfer a residence out of your taxable estate while retaining the right to use it during your lifetime. The gift for federal gift tax purposes is based upon IRS published interest rates at the time of the transfer, and this rate does not take into consideration actual appreciation in the value of the property. Accordingly, these trusts are particularly useful to transfer residences in which significant future appreciation is anticipated.

The Qualified Personal Residence Trust permits you to continue to enjoy your residence, knowing that the value at the date of death will not be included in your estate. During the term of years of the trust, you have the absolute right to remain in the residence rent-free. After the initial term, you can be granted the right to rent the residence for the balance of your lifetime for its fair market rental value. This gives you the opportunity to use other assets in your estate to pay rent and it not be considered a further gift to your children or other family members.

During the term of years, you can be the sole trustee or a co-trustee of the trust with complete control over all decisions of the trust and the assets in the trust. You may also sell the residence and buy another residence during the trust term.

Because the Qualified Personal Residence Trust is a "grantor trust" under the income tax laws, you are treated as the owner of the property for income tax purposes during the initial term of years. Therefore, all items of income, gain, loss and deduction with respect to the trust are treated on your personal income tax return. So for example, the deduction for real estate taxes remains available to you. In addition, favorable capital gains treatment, including capital gain roll-over and the $250,000 individual ($500,000 for a married couple) exclusion of capital gain are still available to you. This strategy is also particularly useful for a vacation home that you wish to keep in the family.

Charitable Trusts

Gifts to charities are fully exempt from gift and estate taxes. In addition, they qualify for current income tax deductions. These lifetime gifts can reduce your estate by both the value of the gift and any subsequent appreciation. Various charitable trusts can be created which offer additional advantages. These trusts, Charitable Remainder Trusts and Charitable Lead Trusts, are discussed below.

Charitable Remainder Trust

The Charitable Remainder Trust ("CRT") is a type of trust specifically authorized by the Internal Revenue Code. These irrevocable trusts permit you to transfer ownership of assets to the trust in exchange for an income stream to the person or persons of your choice (typically you). This can be for life or for a specified term of up to 20 years. With the most common type of Charitable Remainder Trust, at the end of the term, the balance of the trust property (the "remainder interest") is transferred to a specified charity or charities. Charitable Remainder Trusts reduce estate taxes because you transfer ownership to the trust of assets that otherwise would be counted in your estate for estate tax purposes.

A Charitable Remainder Trust can be set up as part of your estate plan. It can come into existence at the time of your death or as a stand-alone trust during your lifetime. At the time of creation of the CRT, you or your estate will be entitled to a charitable deduction in the amount of the current value of the gift that will eventually go to charity. If the income recipient is someone other than you or your spouse, there will be gift tax consequences to the transfer to the CRT.

Charitable Remainder Trusts are tax-exempt entities. In other words, when a Charitable Remainder Trust sells an asset, it pays no income tax on the gain in that asset. Therefore, after a sale, the trust has more available to invest than if the asset were sold outside of the Charitable Remainder Trust and subject to tax. Accordingly, Charitable Remainder Trusts are particularly suited for *highly appreciated assets* such as real estate and stock in a closely held business, or assets subject to income tax such as qualified plans and IRAs. While the Charitable Remainder Trust does not pay tax on the sale of its assets, the tax is not avoided altogether. The payments to the income recipient will be subject to income tax. There are several types of Charitable Remainder Trusts.

> *...when a Charitable Remainder Trust sells an asset, it pays no income tax on the gain in that asset.*

For example, the Charitable Remainder Annuity Trust pays a fixed dollar amount (for example, $80,000 per year) to the income recipient at least annually. Another type of CRT, the Charitable Remainder Unitrust, pays a fixed percentage of the value of the trust assets each year to the income recipient (for example, 5% of the value as of the preceding January 1). A third type, perhaps the most common, allows you to transfer non-income producing property to the CRT. This converts the trust to a Charitable Remainder Unitrust upon the sale or happening of a specified event (for example, upon reaching a specified retirement age). At the end of the term of a Charitable Remainder Trust, the remainder interest passes to qualified charities as defined under the Internal Revenue Code. Generally, any charity that has received IRS tax-exempt status qualifies, but this is not always the case. It is possible for you to name a private foundation established by you as the charitable beneficiary as well.

Charitable Lead Trust

The Charitable Lead Trust is a type of charitable trust that can reduce or virtually eliminate all estate tax on wealth passing to heirs. In order to accomplish this goal, you create a trust that grants a charity or charities the first or "lead" right to receive a payment from the trust, for a set number of years. At the end of the term of years, your children or grandchildren receive the balance of the trust property—which often is greater than the amount contributed— free of estate tax in most instances. Although the Charitable Lead Trust is a complex estate planning strategy, the steps to implement it are few and simple from your perspective.

Here is how one of the most frequently used Charitable Lead Trusts, the Charitable Lead Annuity Trust, operates:

You, as grantors (if you are married), create a Charitable Lead Trust as part of your estate plan. Upon the death of the survivor of the two of you, a substantial amount of property will pass to the Charitable Lead Trust. The income beneficiary of the Charitable Lead Trust will be a qualified charitable organization, chosen by the two of you or by the survivor of you. The charitable income beneficiary receives a fixed, guaranteed amount from the trust for a certain number of years (determined by you with the assistance of your legal and financial advisors). Generally, any charity that has received IRS tax-exempt status qualifies, but this is not always the case.

It is also possible for you to name a private foundation established by you as the charitable beneficiary. The private foundation can be run by your children or grandchildren which can create unity and purpose for the family as a whole. If so, you must have very limited authority over which charity is to receive money from the foundation. Too much control while you are alive will result in adverse tax consequences. At the end of the Charitable Lead Trust's term, the remaining assets in the trust pass to non-charitable trust beneficiaries such as children and grandchildren, free of estate and gift tax. These assets can pass outright to the beneficiaries, or can continue to be held in trust, either in new trusts or in trusts previously established for the benefit and protection of the beneficiaries. The charity will receive the same dollar amount each year, no matter how its investments perform. The remainder interest ultimately passing to the heirs, however, will be affected by the performance of the trust's investments. Charitable Lead Annuity Trusts are particularly suited for hard-to-value assets (such as real estate or family limited liability company interests) and assets which are expected to grow rapidly in value.

It is also possible for you to name a private foundation established by you as the charitable beneficiary.

sixteen

The Top 25 Estate Planning Mistakes People Make and How to Avoid Them

These are the most common mistakes I see in my practice every day. There are many myths and misconceptions out there about estate planning. This chapter will help you recognize and avoid the most common mistakes families make in estate planning and help your family save thousands of dollars in unnecessary taxes and probate fees.

Mistake #1: Not Understanding How Your Assets Will Pass upon Your Death:

Many people think their wills control how all of their assets will pass upon their death. Yet because many people hold much of their wealth in the form of retirement plan accounts or life insurance, many assets today pass outside of wills or trusts. Wills and trusts control real estate and other property that you own, but there are certain assets, like life insurance and IRAs, that are not normally subject to probate and which a will or trust cannot affect. However, note that if you list your trust as the beneficiary of your life insurance, it can be controlled by the terms of your trust (which can include asset protection for your spouse and children if properly drafted).

These assets will pass to the beneficiaries you name in a beneficiary designation form (*however note that a revocable trust can be the beneficiary on these types of accounts with the proper trust provisions—there are many advantages to having your revocable trust as the beneficiary of which we will discuss later in this book).

Example: While still single, Don named his brother as the beneficiary on his retirement plan and his life insurance. Don later got married. After his marriage, Don changed his will to leave everything to his wife. However, because Don never changed his beneficiary designations on his retirement account and life insurance, the bulk of his estate passed to his brother on his death and not to his wife.

This problem can be avoided by reviewing your beneficiary designations for life insurance policies and retirement plans when major life changes happen to make sure they fit your current situation and your estate planning goals.

Mistake #2: Trying To Plan Your Estate Around Specific Assets:

Unless there are compelling reasons why a specific asset should go to a specific person, I strongly discourage clients from trying to plan around specific assets.

Example: Bill had three children and wanted to treat them all equally. His will even confirmed this. Several years before he died, he transferred half of his home to his older son, added his daughter as a signer on his savings account, and named his younger son as the beneficiary on his life insurance policy. When he did this, all three assets were about equal in value. But between these actions and his death, he sold the home, put the proceeds in the savings account, and let the life insurance policy lapse. The savings account passed to the surviving owner and not pursuant to his will. By planning around specific assets, he actually disinherited two of his children! This is not what he intended and this could have easily been avoided with proper planning.

Mistake #3: Failure to Minimize Estate Taxes:

The estate tax exemption, which is the maximum amount you can pass to your heir's estate tax free is $13,610,000 (2024). Many people tell me things like, "My estate is under the exemption - I don't think I will even have a taxable estate." Perhaps they don't want to pay for an estate plan that includes estate tax planning, but they should consider the cost of not planning. Life insurance policies are includable in your estate tax calculation. Many miss this important item in the analysis of the size of their estates. These days, it is not uncommon for me to see clients with $2MM-$4MM or more in term life insurance. Life insurance you own is generally a part of your "taxable" estate calculation. The estate tax could be reduced or avoided with a properly structured estate plan containing the proper tax planning provisions in your revocable trust and possibly other estate planning strategies. Remember that your estate will grow over time, and you need to plan ahead for that. It's also important to note that come January 1, 2026, the federal estate tax exemption will sunset back to the pre-2018 level of $5,000,000 with an index for inflation.

Mistake #4: Relying On Co-Ownership of Property to Avoid Probate:

In California, co-ownership of property does nothing to avoid an eventual probate. At the death of the surviving owner, a probate must be opened. Adding someone to title simply gives them ownership of half the property and can cause tax problems for which you were not aware. For instance, if a mom decides to make her daughter a co-owner so that the property will pass to her daughter upon her death (with right of survivorship), she has accomplished that if the property is in joint tenancy. However, she may have also created a host of tax issues for her daughter as well. The first of which is a reduction in the mother's Federal Estate Tax Exemption because she gave a lifetime gift (if the half of the property was valued greater than $18,000 in the calendar year of the gift—as of 2024).

A second issue is the capital gains tax. Because mom gave half the property to her daughter during her lifetime, the daughter takes her mother's original basis in the half given to her. This could mean a capital gains tax would be due upon the eventual sale of the property on the half given to her. However, if the mother had given the property to her daughter upon death (through a trust) the daughter would have obtained a full step-up in basis to the fair market value of the property at the date of her mother's death. Thus, no capital gains tax would have been due if the property was sold shortly after her mother's death.

A third disadvantage to making her daughter a co-owner is that she opens the door to any potential creditor claims her daughter might have in the future. The property could be subject to a claim and taken to satisfy the debt. As you can see, there are numerous tax and legal implications in the art of estate planning that could be missed by an unskilled person, costing your family big time.

Mistake #5: Losing Control by Adding Someone to Your Bank Accounts:

When you simply add someone's name to your account, you are subjecting that account to his or her creditors. You don't have to be a bad person to be sued these days or to be subject to a tax lien. You may also be inadvertently giving that person an ownership interest in your account (which could affect your gift tax exemption). If you need help managing your finances, you can appoint an agent using a Durable Power of Attorney and give them authority to manage your affairs without exposing your assets to their creditors. You can also use a revocable living trust to achieve the same result by transferring your bank accounts to your trust and listing the person you want to help manage the accounts as either the current trustee of your trust or as a co-trustee with you.

Mistake #6: Putting Your Children on Title to Your House:
When you put your home (or any other asset) in co-ownership with your children, your children become co-owners of the property with you. This causes several problems.

First Problem: Putting your home in joint tenancy with your children is a taxable gift under IRS regulations. This means you have to file a gift tax return for the year in which you made the transfer if the value of the interest transferred to each child is more than $18,000 (2024).

Second Problem: If your child has any lawsuits against him or her, is going through a divorce, or has a tax lien filed against them, you may find out that you no longer own the house with your child, but with your child's creditors. In many jurisdictions, creditors can actually foreclose on (force the sale of) your home to get at your child's fractional share.

Third Problem: When you go to sell the home, you can use your primary residence capital gains exclusion ($250,000 for individuals and up to $500,000 for married couples) only on your fractional share. Each of your children may have a LARGE long-term capital gains tax bill to be paid that could have been totally avoided if the house had still been titled in the name of your revocable trust.

Mistake #7: Failure to Protect a Disabled Beneficiary

If you have a disabled beneficiary, perhaps a handicapped child, you should consider leaving them their inheritance in a specially drafted trust to protect your child and keep them eligible for public assistance. Without public assistance, many such children may have to spend their entire inheritance within a few years on medical and other needs. If you leave the disabled child's inheritance to another child with the understanding that that child would help the disabled child, that child may die, get a divorce, or be sued. This could result in the inheritance not being available to the special needs beneficiary.

Mistake #8: Failure to Make Special Provisions for a "Problem" Child:

After you are gone, will your beneficiaries use their inheritance in a constructive manner? Or will they waste it foolishly? How are they today at managing their money? That may give you some idea as to how their inheritance will be spent after you are gone. Will it be available for the education of your grandchildren, or will it all be gone in just a few years?

Many of my clients come to me liking the idea of holding an inheritance in trust until their beneficiary reaches a certain age, such as 30 years of age. Others like giving their children 1/3 after they are both gone, with another 1/3 in five years, and the last third five years after that. But this gives the beneficiary three chances to blow it! I've even had some clients who are so disillusioned with a child that they have required that the child's share be distributed in monthly payments over 20 years or have decided to asset protect that child's share until that child's death. This could be as strict as not allowing him or her to demand money from the trustee (in this situation, the trustee is in complete charge of giving the beneficiary money for his or her needs).

Other clients have required that their children be tested drug or alcohol free monthly for three years before receiving an inheritance outright. Remember, as long as an inheritance is being held in trust, it can be protected from the beneficiary's spending habits, from creditors, and even from divorcing spouses. Also, your trust can control where the inheritance goes upon the death of the beneficiary. Many of my clients would prefer to see a deceased child's inheritance go to their other children or grandchildren rather than their deceased child's spouse. For more information on lifetime protective trusts, see the prior Chapter 8 on "*Creditor Protection for Your Child's Inheritance*".

Mistake #9: Sloppy Drafting:

Example: John had three children. His will left his estate to "my surviving children." Sounds good, but is that what John meant? If his daughter were deceased, did he really want his estate divided between his other two children, or would he have wanted his deceased daughter's share to pass to her children (his grandchildren)?

Example: Janet's will left her estate equally "to her descendants." At the time she drafted her will, she had two children and no grandchildren. But by the time she died, her son had four children and her daughter none. Under some state laws the term "descendants" includes children, grandchildren, great grandchildren, etc. Thus, by law each descendant gets one-sixth of her estate. Is this what Janet wanted, or do you think she wanted her estate to go half to her son and half to her daughter?

A properly drafted estate plan could have made this clear. For instance, I leave my estate equally to my living descendants; "*per stirpes*" is probably what both John and Janet meant. This language makes it clear that if there are two children, the property is split between the two children. If the daughter is deceased, then her half of the estate will be split equally between her children.

Mistake #10: Trying To "Do It Yourself":

Although the previous example shows how easy it is to botch simple planning, there are many other examples available. John and Mary didn't want to pay an attorney to draft their estate plan, so they bought a living trust kit under which they or the survivor would serve as trustee. In modifying the trust to meet their personal situation, they decided to change the language in the Family Trust which allowed distributions to the surviving spouse for "health, education, maintenance, and support" by adding the words "comfort and welfare". This addition seemed harmless enough to them.

However, the IRS regulations make it very clear that this addition results in the Family Trust being included in the survivor's taxable estate, which was exactly what they were trying to avoid.

Your estate, even if it is modest, still represents big bucks to your spouse and children. Use an experienced estate-planning attorney to make sure that your estate plan and any changes are properly drafted.

Mistake #11: Failing To Realize That Wills Can Be Changed by the Maker:

Jeff and Sara had been married for over 25 years. Each of them had two children by a prior marriage. They wanted to provide for each other first, and then leave the assets equally to all four children. Although their wills stated this intention, the survivor could always change his or her will to leave everything to his or her children only. Or if the survivor's will cannot be found (perhaps destroyed by one of the survivor's children), then all of the assets would pass to the survivor's children.

The use of trusts can help protect children from a prior marriage by either having separate trusts or by having a joint trust listing the assets of each spouse on a separate property schedule. There are also special provisions for sub-trust funding at the death of the first spouse that can be crafted to protect children of a previous marriage. Second marriage planning is often complex and doesn't get the attention it usually deserves, even from many attorneys who supposedly specialize in estate planning.

Mistake #12: Relying On Beneficiary Designations

A beneficiary designation is a very simple form of estate planning which does not handle contingencies very well. For instance, if you name your son and your daughter as the beneficiary on your life insurance policy, and your daughter predeceases you, do you think the insurance company will pay the proceeds all to your son? Or do you think the insurance company will pay your daughter's half of the proceeds to your daughter's children?

Most of us would like to think the later, but most of the beneficiary forms we've seen say just the opposite: The forms usually say "Unless otherwise indicated, we, the insurance company, will pay to the surviving named beneficiaries."

By naming a trust as the beneficiary of your life insurance, your trust can control exactly how the proceeds will be distributed, including such contingencies. The trust can also name a person who will manage and distribute the money for minor children or grandchildren.

Mistake #13: Trying To Leave Property to a Minor Child or Grandchild:

No insurance company will knowingly pay $500,000 to a twelve-year-old. They will only pay it to a court-appointed guardian for that child, who may not be the person you would want. The cost of obtaining such a court order can also be substantial.

Example: Your will or beneficiary designation indicates that your deceased daughter's share is to go to her children. If they are minors, a guardian will need to be appointed by the court. The court would give priority to the children's father, who may be your ex-son-in-law.

Generally, in a guardianship, the money is required to be turned over to the minor once he or she reaches 18 years of age. That age is perhaps one of the worst ages to turn over a significant inheritance to a child or grandchild. An inheritance left in trust for such a beneficiary can specifically indicate who is going to manage the funds and make distributions for college and the like. It can also indicate the age at which the funds will be turned over to the beneficiary or when the child could become the trustee of their own trust. For instance, in many trusts that I draft, I encourage my clients to select a trustee that is an independent trustee (a successor trustee that is not related to or subordinate to them or their children). With an independent trustee in place, a court CANNOT force a distribution from that child's continuing trust.

Remember, as long as the inheritance is held in trust with an independent Trustee in charge, it can be protected from:

- your child's bad spending habits

- your child's future divorcing spouse

- your child's creditors or lawsuits lodged against them

A properly structured continuing trust can also indicate who receives the inheritance in the event of your child's death, and with proper investment, the inheritance can grow, providing more financial support over time.

Mistake #14: Failure to Consider Who Pays Estate Taxes:

John drafted his trust to leave his home to go to his companion of many years and the remainder of his estate to go to his children. However, he and his attorney never discussed who would pay the estate taxes, and his trust said (as many trusts do) that taxes and expenses would be paid out of the "residuary estate," that is, from the remainder distribution after specific distributions.

Therefore, on John's death, the estate taxes will be paid solely out of assets which pass pursuant to the residuary clause of his trust, and therefore, out of his children's inheritance.

In this extreme example, the home was worth $5 million and the remaining assets were worth $5 million. The estate taxes were $4,430,000 (in 2003) and the expenses were $70,000, so the kids received only $500,000, while the companion walked away with the $5 million palatial home estate tax free. We doubt that is what John would have wanted if he had considered who pays the estate taxes.

Many trusts say, "pay all taxes out of the residuary estate." Phrases like that sound good but may not be what you want unless you fully understand exactly what they mean.

Mistake #15: Failure to Consider the Income Tax Aspects of Your Assets:

Marlene's two major assets were her life insurance and her (traditional) IRA; and they were of equal value. So, she named her son as the beneficiary on the life insurance, and named her daughter as the beneficiary on her IRA. The proceeds of life insurance are income tax free, but the proceeds from an IRA are generally all subject to income tax. The daughter lost approximately one-third of the proceeds to income taxes.

This is one of the reasons we discourage our clients from leaving specific assets to specific persons. Consider naming all children as beneficiaries, or better yet, leaving all assets to your trust, with the trust dividing them equally and providing who will receive what in the event a child should predecease you.

Mistake #16: Failure to Consider All the Tax Consequences of a Gift:

Mary was diagnosed with terminal cancer. She had heard that probate could cost her children thousands of dollars. She heard that probate could be avoided by deeding her home to her kids while she was alive. Luckily, none of the problems we previously discussed developed, such as a child's divorce, lawsuits, tax liens, etc. while Mary was alive. But when the kids sold Mary's home after her death for $500,000, they discovered that their "basis" (cost for determining taxable gain) was Mom's cost 30 years ago, which was $50,000. The taxable gain was $450,000 and over 30% (the federal and state tax on the capital gain at the time), the tax was over $130,000.

Their accountant correctly informed them that if Mary had owned the property on her death (or if it were owned by her living trust), then the children would have inherited it with a "step up in basis". That means that their basis (or cost for determining taxable gain) would have been the fair market value on Mary's date of death ($500,000). There would have been no capital gains tax payable on the sale shortly after Mary's death. Mary's gift to avoid probate cost her children $130,000! If the children had acquired the home on Mary's death (and not by gift during her lifetime) and did not sell it, but rented it out, they also could have taken depreciation based upon its fair market value on their mother's date of death.

Mistake #17: Using the Wrong Assets to Fund a Gift to Charity:

Mark wanted to leave $100,000 to his church upon his death, and the rest to his children. Mark's attorney was inexperienced in estate planning, and but for a very reasonable fee drafted Mark's trust as instructed: "$100,000 to my church and the balance equally to my children." Mark's large IRA passed to his children, who had to pay income tax on it.

Had Mark funded the charitable bequest with his IRA, there would have been $100,000 less taxable income to the children, increasing the amount that passed to them after income taxes by, perhaps, $40,000 (at a 40% rate for both federal and state income taxes). Charities don't care if they receive taxable income property because they don't pay income taxes anyway. Michael saved a few dollars on the drafting side which later, in effect, cost his children $40,000.

Mistake #18: Failure to Fund Your Living Trust:

Bob and Carol had a Living Trust but neglected to re-title their assets as instructed by their attorney. The attorney even deeded their home to their trust, but they later sold the home and purchased another home in their personal names and not in the name of the trust. Bob died a few years ago, and on Carol's death, all of the assets were subject to probate and were part of her taxable estate. By not titling their assets in the name of their trust, they defeated two of their planning goals: avoiding probate and reducing estate taxes.

Moral: If you have a living trust, be sure to fund it with your assets by changing record title or beneficiary designations as instructed by your attorney. Or better yet, hire an attorney that offers this as an option in their legal services.

Mistake #19: Not Contacting an Attorney after the Death of the First Spouse:

I've seen time and time again instances where a surviving spouse has not contacted an attorney to help with the trust administration after the death of their spouse. The most common situation where this can spell big trouble is if the couple had an A/B type trust. Upon the death of the first spouse, the trust property is to be split (according to the formula laid out in the trust document) into an "A" trust for the surviving spouse (which remains revocable by the surviving spouse) and a "B" trust which holds the decedent's half of the estate. This is usually in an irrevocable trust for the benefit of the children, passed to them at the death of the surviving spouse.

Many times, however, the surviving spouse subsequently becomes incapacitated and the baton is passed to the successor trustee. The successor trustee steps in and tries to understand how to deal with the trust and if they are smart, they end up talking to an experienced estate planning and trust administration attorney. What they often find out is that the surviving spouse did not do what they should have. This creates a legal and accounting nightmare for the successor trustee. We then have to try to "fix" the problems that have arisen from the improper or lack of trust administration by the surviving spouse. This ends up costing the family a lot more money than if the surviving spouse had simply contacted an experienced trust administration attorney to set up the trust split when the first spouse died.

The moral of the story is to seek help and never assume that a trust administration will be simple (it might be but you always want to check with an attorney to ensure things are being properly administered).

Mistake #20: Missing a Disclaimer Deadline:

A disclaimer is a refusal to accept an inheritance. A qualified disclaimer is one that complies with IRS and state law requirements, one of which requires that the disclaimer be made in writing within nine months of the decedent's death.

So why would someone want to disclaim an inheritance? Let's say a couple has a taxable estate and holds considerable property. The wife dies. If the husband disclaims his wife's half, her half will pass to their children. Or, if the couple has a properly drafted Living Trust, it could pass to a Credit Shelter Trust for the benefit of the surviving spouse and then later pass to the children. If the disclaimer is made pursuant to IRS regulations, the disclaimer is not treated as a taxable gift.

Example: Michael was in poor health when his wife died in 2006. Their combined estate was $4.0 million. They each had a simple will leaving everything to the other, a sound plan so they thought. However, if Michael had executed a qualified disclaimer within nine months of his wife's death, her half of the estate would have passed to their children instead of him and would not have been treated as a taxable gift by Michael. If Michael then died in 2008, no estate taxes would have been due.

This could have also been accomplished by having a trust with an optional disclaimer sub-trust provision built in. However, because Michael missed the deadline, his wife's half of their assets was included in his taxable estate, and on his death in 2008, the estate taxes were $900,000 - all of which could have been avoided if Michael had made the qualified disclaimer.

Qualified disclaimers are an important planning tool in many estates. In fact, many estate plans are designed to anticipate the use of disclaimers for saving on estate taxes. Disclaimers are just one of the many reasons why it is important to see an experienced and knowledgeable estate planning attorney to plan ahead to minimize or eliminate your estate taxes.

Mistake #21: Not Doing an Estate Plan While Divorce Is Pending:

If you get a divorce, in most states your ex-spouse is automatically disinherited from your will. But what if you die before the divorce is final? In that case your soon-to-be ex-spouse will still inherit under your will or trust. Therefore, it is very important to change or amend your estate plan as soon as a divorce is filed.

Many people will usually wait until the divorce is final, which, by then, is often far less important. Also keep in mind that a divorce decree does not automatically change beneficiary designations, such as on life insurance and qualified retirement plans. You must file a change of beneficiary designation form.

Mistake #22: Failure to Have Proper Beneficiary Designations on Your IRA:

After his wife died, Fred was advised to name his three children as the beneficiaries on his IRA. He assured us that he had already done so (or that they were the contingent beneficiaries).

On Fred's death, it was discovered that he had never made the change and that the original beneficiary form had only named his (predeceased) wife as the beneficiary. His IRA agreement with the custodian stated that if there is no surviving beneficiary designated, the IRA would be paid to his estate.

Although that provision still gets the IRA to his children through a probate, it means that they have to liquidate the IRA in a very short period of time, creating a greater tax liability because income tax will be due on the IRA.

Had he named the children on the IRA beneficiary form, the children could have deferred withdrawal of the income for up to ten (10) years, allowing it to continue to compound tax deferred. Fred's small IRA could have actually funded his kids' education or retirement had he named them as beneficiaries.

Therefore, it is very important to VERIFY your beneficiary designations (or file a new form) and NOT depend on your memory.

Mistake #23: Failure to Have Gifting Powers in Your Power Of Attorney:

Harold was on his deathbed. His son knew Harold had a taxable estate, so Harold's son, acting under a Durable Power of Attorney, made gifts of $18,000 (the annual gift exclusion amount in 2024) each from Harold to his 5 children and their spouses.

This gifting had the potential of removing $180,000 from Harold's taxable estate, saving at least $72,000 in estate taxes. But the IRS ruled that because Harold's Power of Attorney did not specifically grant his son the power to make those gifts, his son operated in violation of the law, and the IRS deemed the gifts incomplete.

A Power of Attorney generally does not give the agent the authority to give away your assets. The agent is supposed to operate in your best interests. If Harold had a legal right to recover the gifts, the IRS will include them in Harold's taxable estate. The omission of gifting provisions in the Power of Attorney cost this family over $72,000.

The moral of the story: If appropriate, be sure your power of attorney contains specific gifting provisions.

Mistake #24: Assuming That All Estate Plans Are Equal:

I have seen many poorly drafted Trust-based estate plans drafted by inexperienced attorneys and even some drafted by financial planners and CPAs.

Some revocable living trusts will not even avoid probate, as such trusts say, "Upon my death my trust shall be paid to my estate." Many trusts drafted for married couples don't even have estate tax planning provisions.

A trust can be as short or as long as you want to make it. There is no such thing as a "standard living trust." A one-page trust might technically be a valid trust, but it probably does not do most of the things it should do that we have discussed in this book.

Assuming that all estate plans are basically the same can be a costly error. If you have any doubts, we suggest getting your estate plan reviewed by an experienced attorney.

Mistake #25: Not Having an Estate Plan At All!:

If you don't have an estate plan, most states have one for you, and it may not be what you would want. Not many people would purposely let their state legislature draft their estate plan for them, yet that is what you get if you don't plan yourself.

For instance, under California law, if you are married with children, your property could go to your children and your spouse proportionally if you have no plan. We find that is rarely what our married clients want. Most couples want to give more control over their assets to their surviving spouse and see their kids get an inheritance only after they are both gone. One of my Probate clients had this happen to her and her minor children. Their house and several investment accounts were titled in her husband's name alone. According to the Probate Code, two-thirds of his property passed to his two minor children and one-third to his wife. No matter what she knew his intent to be, that is what the law required because they had no estate plan in place.

...under California law, if you are married with children, your property could go to your children and your spouse proportionally if you have no plan.

seventeen

What to Do Next?

Now that you've read this book and know quite a bit about Estate Planning, the next step is to call our office at (760) 448-2220 and request your estate planning design meeting with one of our attorneys.

We will then send you our welcome package by priority mail that will include a brief questionnaire, directions to our office, our client process roadmap, your attorney's bio, several articles I've written specific to your situation, and a letter that confirms your appointment time in-person, by Zoom or via conference call.

We will then text you three days before and call you the day before your appointment to confirm. Your design meeting will likely last about one hour. At the end of that meeting, your attorney should have enough information to draft your estate plan and we will schedule your Estate Plan signing (typically 3-4 weeks later).

At the end of your trust signing meeting with one of our legal assistant notaries, in most cases we will schedule a third meeting with you, which is your "funding" meeting. This is where we deliver all of your signed documents back to you in a custom binder after we've had a chance to scan everything you've signed, record any real property deeds, and prepare your funding letter to aide you with your banks, financial institutions, retirement accounts and life insurance policies.

We look forward to hearing from you and providing you and your family state of-the-art legal services and outstanding client service. For more valuable information on estate, elder or business planning, go to www.geigerlawoffice.com. We have a ton of blog posts, FAQs, articles, videos, and radio & TV interviews to help you on your road to properly protecting your family.

eighteen

About the Author

BRENDA GEIGER, J.D.
Managing Attorney, Geiger Law Office, P.C.

Brenda Geiger is the Founder and Managing Attorney of Geiger Law Office, P.C. Geiger Law Office, P.C., a Trusts & Estates law firm which began in 2007 in North County San Diego. The firm has helped over 5,000 families to protect themselves and their families through innova-  tive estate and asset protection strategies and has additional office locations in Orange County and San Diego County.

While studying at the University of San Diego School of Law, Brenda was honored to be selected for the Oxford University International Comparative Law Program in Oxford, England and was also a member of the Entrepreneurship Clinic and San Diego International Law Journal.

Brenda is the author of six other books including *Safeguarding the Nest, Fourth Edition; Protecting an Aging Parent from a Long-Term Care Financial Crisis; Protecting Your Children's IRA Inheritance with a Retirement Protector Trust, Second Edition; Protecting You and Your Business; Estate Planning Secrets of the Affluent, Third Edition;* and *The Trustee's Guide to Trust Administration in California;* and a law review article published in 2003 in the San Diego International Law Journal.

Brenda is also a sought-after speaker and attorney coach for Atticus Advantage. She has been featured on KPBS, NBC, KFMB 760, ESPN 1700, Real Talk San Diego, North County Lawyer Magazine, Wealth Counsel Quarterly Magazine, and the San Diego International Law Journal.

On a more personal note, Brenda grew up in the mid-west, married the love of her life Len, a former Marine Corps officer in 2004, and has a son and a daughter that she loves to spend time with. The Geigers love adventure, soccer and travel and look forward to many more years of it.

You can connect with Brenda at www.geigerlawoffice.com or at https://www.linkedin.com/in/brendageiger/.

GEIGER LAW OFFICE, P.C.

1917 Palomar Oaks Way, Suite 160
Carlsbad, CA 92008

and

32451 Golden Lantern, Suite 307
Laguna Niguel, CA 92677

(949) 769-2440

www.geigerlawoffice.com

WA

Made in the USA
Middletown, DE
01 September 2024

60237386R00080